Military Government and Popular Participation in Panama

Westview Special Studies

The concept of Westview Special Studies is a response to the continuing crisis in academic and informational publishing. Library budgets are being diverted from the purchase of books and used for data banks, computers, micromedia, and other methods of information retrieval. Interlibrary loan structures further reduce the edition sizes required to satisfy the needs of the scholarly community. Economic pressures on university presses and the few private scholarly publishing companies have greatly limited the capacity of the industry to properly serve the academic and research communities. As a result, many manuscripts dealing with important subjects, often representing the highest level of scholarship, are no longer economically viable publishing projects--or, if accepted for publication, are typically subject to lead times ranging from one to three years.

Westview Special Studies are our practical solution to the problem. As always, the selection criteria include the importance of the subject, the work's contribution to scholarship, and its insight, originality of thought, and excellence of exposition. We accept manuscripts in camera-ready form, typed, set, or word processed according to specifications laid out in our comprehensive manual, which contains straightforward instructions and sample pages. The responsibility for editing and proofreading lies with the author or sponsoring institution, but our editorial staff is always available to answer questions and provide guidance.

The result is a book printed on acid-free paper and bound in sturdy library-quality soft covers. We manufacture these books ourselves using equipment that does not require a lengthy make-ready process and that allows us to publish first editions of 300 to 1000 copies and to reprint even smaller quantities as needed. Thus, we can produce Special Studies quickly and can keep even very specialized books in print as long as there is a demand for them.

About the Book and Author

This study details the formation of a populist alliance by the Panamanian military in order to legitimize its leadership and restructure the rules of the political process. Along with the move for popular support, the Torrijos regime introduced an economic strategy based on export-oriented industrialization. The shift toward such policies by General Omar Torrijos Herrera, whose ideologies and political strategies were "neither the left nor the right," bewildered and confused many in Panama and the United States, especially groups accustomed to having their vested interests coincide with those of the Panamanian military. The lessons drawn from this study illustrate an alternative to exclusionary and repressive military regimes in Central America.

George Priestley is assistant professor of political science and chairman of the Latin America Area Studies Program at Queens College, New York.

Military Government and Popular Participation in Panama

The Torrijos Regime, 1968–1975

George Priestley

Routledge
Taylor & Francis Group
LONDON AND NEW YORK

First published 1986 by Westview Press

Published 2018 by Routledge
52 Vanderbilt Avenue, New York, NY 10017
2 Park Square, Milton Park, Abingdon, Oxon OX14 4RN

Routledge is an imprint of the Taylor & Francis Group, an informa business

Priestley, George.
Military government and popular participation in Panama.

(Westview special studies on Latin America and the Caribbean)
Bibliography: p.
Includes index.
1. Panama--Politics and government--1946-
2. Torrijos Herrera, Omar, 1926- --Political and social views. 3. Political participation--Panama--History--20th century. 4. Military government--Panama--History--20th century. I. Title.
F1567.P74 1986 972.87′052 85-3168
ISBN 0-8133-7045-0

ISBN 13: 978-0-367-00877-2 (hbk)

ISBN 13: 978-0-367-15864-4 (pbk)

Contents

Acknowledgments

Obviously there are too few pages to extend my thanks to all those who have contributed to this book. However, there are a few without whose help the completion of this manuscript would have been impossible. Alice Priestley, my mother, encouraged me in my intellectual pursuits until the day she passed away, January 21, 1978. Without the dedication and immense sacrifice of my wife, Marva, the task would have been simply impossible. Amilcar, my seven-year-old, showed unusual comprehension as I absented myself for weeks at a time.

In Panama, Marco Gandasegui provided me with everything: he was a friend, a critic, and a source of information. He is one of Panama's most outstanding social scientists, and to him I remain forever indebted. I am equally indebted to all the young scholars who returned to Panama in the 1970s and who enriched Panama's political literature with their writings, manuscripts, and debates, particularly Simeon Gonzalez, Egbert Wetherborne, Juan Jovane, Gerardo Maloney, Javier Gorostiaga, Omar Jaen Suarez, Ricaurte Soler, Hildebrando Araica, and Graciela Dixon. I also extend thanks to Roberto and Mita Mears who provided me with valuable support and a home base from which to operate from 1973 through 1975.

To all those humble men and women who served in the National Assembly of Community Representatives, asentamientos campesinos (small-scale production settlements), juntas agrarias (agrarian production cooperative ventures), and health committees and who spent countless hours educating me as to the "realidad Panamena," I say thank you.

In New York, Prof. Douglas Chalmers, chairman of the Political Science Department at Columbia University, spent countless hours reading earlier and later drafts. Without his patience and commitment, I would not have completed this book. My colleague Ronald Schneider of Queens College read several drafts and made valuable comments. Humberto Brown, Carolyn Brown, Omayemi Agbeyegbe, Alem Habtu, and Monica Jardim all helped in reading and criticizing earlier versions. Terry Carmichael, in Canada, edited a few chapters of an earlier draft. My colleague Juan Flores of Queens College read the latest draft and offered invaluable theoretical insights on Gramsci's works. Last but not least, Stefan Kass, a friend and critic, read the manuscript, challenged many assumptions, and provided me with invaluable theoretical and historical insights on Bonapartism.

Palmira Rios and Eduardo Vega offered many helpful suggestions and technical assistance. Judy Butler, editor of NACLA, edited an earlier version of the book, and Dolores Schaefer typed it. The colossal task of editing this book, however, was undertaken by Martha and Richard Bush. Martha and Richard, thank you very much. Much thanks is also owed to Westview's editor Krista Hayenga, who while being tough, provided me with a "torch" to see the light at the end of the tunnel.

For the better part of 1985 my staff and friends at Queens College Latin American Area Studies have shared with me the anxiety and burdens of producing the final draft of this manuscript. To all of them--Raul, Segundo, Gloria, Liliana, and David--thank you. Special thanks goes to my assistant, Adriana Conde, for her efficiency and understanding in my most difficult moments.

It goes without saying, however, that I remain exclusively responsible for the contents and interpretation of this book.

George Priestley

1

Introduction

In October 1968 the Panamanian military executed a coup d'etat against the civilian government. Under the leadership of General Omar Torrijos, who quickly emerged as the dominant figure of the regime, the military government introduced radical and significant changes in the country's political and economic life.

These innovations set Panama's National Guard apart from its interventionist counterparts in other Central and South American countries. Politically, Torrijos went beyond abolishing traditional, liberal institutions like the National Assembly and political parties and enacted a constitution that concentrated legislative and executive powers in the hands of the military. He created various mechanisms for popular participation by the previously excluded working classes.

Economically, Torrijos retained the private sector's primary role in production and distribution. In addition, however, the state became a significant actor in the economy, through the creation of a variety of public enterprises, particularly in banking and finance, and through the promulgation of a labor code that favored the interests of workers.

The military regime's boldest initiatives came in foreign policy, specifically with respect to the United States, which held Panama in a semicolonial status. Torrijos rejected U.S. proposals to resolve the conflict over the Panama Canal. He demanded that the United States evacuate the military base at Rio Hato in Cocle province, and, in 1973, went so far as to convene the United Nations Security Council in Panama to put pressure on the Nixon administration to reopen negotiations on a canal treaty.

The structure and policies of the Torrijos regime were intriguing in several respects. In the first place, they went against the conservative grain of previous Panamanian governments with respect to social reform and canal negotiations. Second, they differed dramatically from the style of rule of other military regimes in Central America. Whereas Anastasio Somoza, for example, chose to close off channels of mass participation, Torrijos dared to open them up. Third, Panama's October Revolution calls into question the prevailing explanations of why the military intervenes in politics.

This study examines the first seven years of Torrijos's military government, with particular attention to its efforts to build political institutions appropriate to the dynamics of class relations within Panama and the country's evolving dependency on the United States. This first chapter sets the scene, in a theoretical, sociological, and historical sense. Chapter 2 describes the conditions that prompted the October Revolution, Torrijos's emergence as the dominant figure in the military government, and its central policies. Chapter 3 examines how the military government sought to implement its political program in a selected urban area, the squatter district of San Miguelito. Chapter 4 analyzes the condition of the rural sector, primarily the landless peasantry and its relationship to their self-styled defender, the Bonapartist Torrijos. Chapters 5, 6, and 7 offer a detailed review of how Torrijos attempted to restructure the systems of representation and legitimization.

Theoretical Frameworks

Of the recent discussions of praetorianism in modern Latin America, Amos Perlmutter's is probably the most influential. He attributes military interventionism to the corporate interests of the armed forces and not to their status as experts or bureaucrats.[1] As the disciplinarian/ruler and the state's major defender, Perlmutter argues, the military acts to correct perceived or actual inefficiencies, corruption, instability, and radicalism in civil society.[2] The military rulers, argues Perlmutter, lack experience and motivation to secure popular support. Even in the event that they do so, legitimacy does not follow.[3]

There are several weaknesses in Perlmutter's approach that dilute its utility for understanding the Panamanian case. In the first place, he equivocates on the relationship between corporatism and professionalism in the military in Third World countries. He argues that "military corporatism is both a bulwark against intervention, and, in different times and regimes, a stimulant for it."[4] Moreover, he constructs a model wherein the military is torn between the two tendencies of disciplinarian/ruler and expert/bureaucrat. That begs the question of whether corporatism can lead to professionalism, which in turn serves as a bulwark against military intervention.

Second, Perlmutter dismisses out of hand the possibility that a military regime can garner support and legitimacy for itself. As we will demonstrate in later chapters, the Torrijos regime enjoyed substantial popular support during the 1968-75 period, which assured its legitimacy.

Finally, we disagree with Perlmutter's conclusion that Latin America is faced with a choice between a praetorian army acting as a military dictatorship or a revolutionary regime acting through the army.[5] This either/or formulation suggests that Latin America is irretrievably caught up in the East-West conflict. But it discounts the quest of all of Latin America for social and political democracy and its struggle for national liberation. And it does not explain the exceptional case of Panama under Torrijos.

More useful than looking within the military at its values, norms, and institutional interests is to focus on the dynamics of the society with which it is interacting. In this regard, the approach of Mario Esteban Carranza is particularly insightful.[6] He finds the seeds of military intervention in the ideological, political, and economic crises that can affect states under the circumstances of the imperialist stage of capitalism.

Key to Carranza's approach is the concept of political hegemony in civil society. As stated by Robert Jessop, political hegemony exists when:

--the dominant social classes take into account systematically the popular interest and organize popular support for the attainment of national goals that simultaneously serve the fundamental, long-term interests of the dominant group.

--the dominant classes exercise intellectual and moral leadership, which is necessary in forming and reproducing a collective will--a "national-popular" outlook adequate to the needs of social and economic reproduction.[7]

When the dominant classes fail to meet these conditions, there exists a "crisis of hegemony." This fosters the emergence of what Carranza calls the "state of exception," in which the military penetrates civil society to reconstitute political hegemony. In effect, the military assumes the role of political parties, by trying to provide political and ideological coherence to the dominant classes. For example, the military regime may introduce educational, political, and social reforms, and propagate a nationalistic or populist ideology in order to construct a new legitimacy.

As elucidated by Carranza, the "state of exception" can take one of three possible forms--pure military government, Bonapartism, and fascism--depending on external and internal circumstances. Thus, Bonapartist regimes emerged in Peru and Panama, whereas the fascist variant was the rule in Chile.

Bonapartism as a Leadership Style. The central element of Bonapartism is the ability of the leader to "rise above" all classes and establish some autonomy for the state. The seminal discussion was, of course, that of Karl Marx in his Eighteenth Brumaire of Louis Bonaparte. The phenomenon was later elaborated by Leon Trotsky in his Russian Revolution.[8] As Trotsky analyzed the impasse in the "July government" of Kerensky:

> The design had been a common consent to establish above the democracy and the bourgeoisie, who were paralyzing each other, a "real" sovereign power. This idea of a master of destiny rising above all classes is nothing but Bonapartism. 9

According to Trotsky, Kerensky failed in his Bonapartist role because he was confronted by a "great revolution which had not yet solved its problems or exhausted its force."[10] Bismarck, on the other hand, had succeeded in standing "above classes" because his rule offered a solution, or a half solution, to such a mighty national problem as the unification of Germany.[11]

Hal Draper, in his Karl Marx's Theory of Revolution, elaborates the principal elements of Bonapartism:

1. The historical role of the Bonapartist state is the modernization of society.

2. In the Bonapartist state, the bourgeoisie trades its political rights and power in exchange for the assurance of economic expansion.

3. The Bonapartist state has to enforce the interests of a class even against the opposition of the class itself or against its unenlightened sections.

4. Bonapartism as a state form does not depend on the personal qualities of the dictator in charge.

5. The crux of Bonapartism is the autonomization of state power with respect to all classes, including the ruling class.

6. The objective historical result of a Bonapartist state is a social transformation, a "revolution from above."[12]

One implication of this description of the Bonapartist state is that, because it is not the captive of the ruling class, it may well act in ways that benefit the heterogeneous middle class, from which many military officers come. Bernardo Sorj's analysis of military reformism in Peru after 1968 is particularly relevant. He stresses that "every political regime enjoys an appreciable field of relatively autonomous action," even though the regime in question may be made up of organizations that were originally rooted in particular social classes. Thus in the wake of a coup, it is necessary to identify the specific responses of the officer corps to the class struggles and ideological conflicts to see which classes the military's political projects benefit. It may well be secondary (i.e., middle) classes,[13] in which case the military can in effect alter the mode of accumulation, distribution, and power relations in a specific social formation.

Panama under Torrijos

In light of this theoretical discussion, let us describe in summary fashion our interpretation of Panama under Torrijos. The Panamanian military came to power in 1968 as a result of a crisis in hegemony. The civilian oligarchy was morally and intellectually bankrupt. It was incapable of containing the social conflict that stemmed from the specific class structure of Panamanian society. And it was impotent in securing the end of the U.S. colonial presence in the Panama Canal Zone.

Once in power, Torrijos enjoyed a significant autonomous political action. Displaying a Bonapartist leadership style, he engineered significant innovations in the country's political life. His regime was corporatist in the sense that it created institutions designed to incorporate urban workers, peasants, and the student movement into politics without losing control over the process. This revolution from above was made possible by the populist political discourse--simultaneously anti-oligarchy and anti-American--and in turn altered class relations within Panama and Panama's relationship with the United States.

Furthermore, the regime sought to institutionalize its rule by promulgating a new constitution that centralized power in the hands of the executive while creating structures for political participation at the local level.

The Social Setting

In 1974, toward the end of the period covered in this study, Panama was a nation of 1.7 million people. The population grew rapidly (3 percent per year in 1970), and was relatively young--40 percent under the age of fifteen.[14] It was also a predominantly urban society: 48 percent of the population lived in urban areas, mostly in the province of Panama and Panama City. As the primary city, Panama City contained the greatest concentration of the nation's wealth and infrastructure.[15]

Key to an understanding of Panama's contemporary politics **is an understanding of the historical relationship between color and ethnicity on the one hand, and social class on the other.** Colonial society was composed of a minority of Spaniards, known as *penisulares* and *criollos*, Indians, and blacks. The indigenous population worked lands owned by Spaniards in the interior provinces. Black slaves provided the labor power for the mines and for transportation along transit routes, and, along with mulattoes, constituted the majority of urban residents. Thus in 1789, toward the end of the colonial period, the province of Panama had 7,951 whites, 19,702 free blacks, 2,793 black slaves, and 9 mulattoes.[16]

The proportion of blacks in the population as a whole and in Panama City increased after Panama traded its colonial status under Spain for a semicolonial relationship with Colombia. Caribbean blacks came in three migratory waves, in response to major construction projects on the isthmus. The first was the Panama Railroad, begun in 1850. During the 1880s, blacks from Martinique and Guadaloupe came to work on the French canal project. And, after 1900, more came from Barbados, Guadaloupe, and Martinique to build the Panama Canal.[17] **Velma Newton estimates that approximately 63,800 blacks migrated to Panama between 1850 and 1915.**[18] Other estimates range as high as 100,000. Whatever the number, their presence served to exacerbate social and political tensions between the dominant white oligarchy and the popular classes.[19] It should be no surprise, therefore, that in the 1940s President Arnulfo Arias advocated an exclusionary type of nationalism: the constitution he drafted denied Panamanian citizenship to Caribbean blacks, Chinese, Hindus, and other nonwhite immigrants.

Social Classes

The Panamanian social structure, which took final shape in the early twentieth century, was composed of four classes:

--a predominantly white economic and political oligarchy.

--a racially mixed middle class that was dependent on the oligarchy economically and imitated it culturally, but which was to post challenges to it politically.

--the mulatto, mestizo, and black popular sectors who constituted the majority of the urban population.

--and peasants and farmers.

The Oligarchy. This dominant bloc is made up of three main groups: the commercial and real estate bourgeoisie, the landowning bourgeoisie, and the Modernizing Entrepreneurs. The commercial and real estate bourgeoisie engages in import-export and retailing, housing, rentals, warehousing, and so on, while the landowning bourgeoisie is involved in cattle breeding and in money lending to small and medium farmers. The Modernizing Entrepreneurs, consisting mainly of immigrant whites from Europe and the United States, were pioneers and the pillar of Panama's industrial efforts. They control important industries such as the National Brewery, the National Sugar Company, Compania Panamena de Aceites, Compania Chiricana de Leche, Cemento Panama, and many banks and finance companies.[20]

It is the oligarchy, and especially its real estate and commercial members, that exercised political power for almost seven decades prior to the 1968 military coup. Moreover, its control and influence over civil institutions such as the church, the media, and the schools allowed the oligarchy considerable social power over the subordinate classes. This social power expressed itself both in civil society as well as in the state. In civil society its highest organized expression is in the National Confederation of Private Enterprise (CONEP) and in exclusive and exclusionary social clubs such as the Union Club. Its political rule is organized through nonprogrammatic and highly personalist political parties, each of which claims roots in the liberal tradition.

<u>The Middle Class</u>. Although the concept of middle class is imprecise, we will use the term to refer primarily to the urban intellectuals, professionals, teachers, lawyers, and upper-income employees in the state bureaucracy.

The origins and growth of this class are due to the dominance of the service sector in Panama's economy. In addition to generating low-paying, nonproductive work, this service sector generates and reproduces the need for lawyers, bureaucrats, and professionals of various kinds. But this fact aside, the middle class was historically locked out of business opportunities by the oligarchy and its European and American partners and therefore turned to education and professional politics for upward mobility.

The role of the middle class, especially that of teachers, has been important in Panamanian politics since at least the 1930s. Renato Pereira suggests that the oligarchical state devised a strategy of incorporating members of the middle class by adopting a liberal and inclusionary educational policy. For example, in 1935 President Harmodio Arias Madrid, in collaboration with Dr. Octavio Mendez Pereira, founded the University of Panama.[21] Subsequent administrations built scores of secondary schools, which increased enrollment by leaps and bounds. As a result, in the 1940s several educational-based institutions--such as the Federation of Panamanian Students (FEP), United Panamanian Teachers Association, and the Secondary Schools Teachers Association--were formed. These organizations, and especially FEP, have played and continue to play important roles in Panamanian politics.

<u>The Popular Class</u>. This class comprises the bulk of the low-paid employees in the private and public sectors: banana workers, most Canal Zone employees, and a small sector of construction and production workers. Herbert de Souza, referring to the majority of employees in Panama, said that "considering society as a whole, one may speak of a large majority of 'salaried' employees, who live in an economic and social condition of low incomes, terrible living conditions and high unemployment rates. But, by virtue of their situation in the productive structure and the interests and aspirations generated there, one cannot speak of a 'proletarian' majority with all its political consequences."[22] In spite of Souza's characterization, there are pockets of production workers in Panama, located primarily but not exclusively in the foreign-dominated Canal Zone and

banana enclaves and to a lesser extent in the construction and industrial manufacturing sectors.

The workers in the manufacturing industry are dispersed in many small- and medium-sized industries and in 1972 contributed only 16 percent to the GNP while absorbing 24 percent of jobs in the private sector. In the same year, the construction industry had 12,000 workers or 11.9 percent of the private sector.

Commercial employees number over 30,000 and constitute 37.5 percent of private sector employees. They work mainly in the retail stores along the principal avenues in Panama City.

In 1972 the transportation work force was made up of less than 1000 bus drivers servicing Panama and Colon cities. Until 1972, when they were re-organized as employees under the new labor code, they were considered to be tenants. They had no salaries and received no fringe benefits, but got to keep that part of the fare collected after paying several rental fees to the bus owner. The role of the bus workers in politics was crucial in the 1950s and early 1960s when, in support of working class and popular struggles, they struck and paralyzed the cities of Colon and Panama.

In 1971 there were over 14,000 banana workers, mostly blacks of Caribbean descent and Guaymi natives, employed by United Brands in the provinces of Bocas del Toro and Chiriqui. Because this industry is important to Panama's export (representing in 1972, 53 percent of agricultural exports or $64 million dollars) and because banana workers labor under some of the worst conditions and are among the worst paid on the isthmus, the industry has suffered incessant labor-management conflicts. In the 1960s the workers threw off the company unions and organized independent unions. These unions, under the leadership of progressives, socialists, and communists, struck United Fruit (now United Brands) repeatedly, confronting the economic power of the company and the repressive policies of the oligarchical regimes of Chiari and Robles. There is no doubt that the banana workers union served as the spark of the labor movement of the 1960s. Their support in 1969 was crucial to the success of Torrijos's strategy of organizing a populist alliance.

The Canal Zone workers, largely of Caribbean descent, numbered about 14,000 in 1972. The average salary in this sector in 1972 was $420 per month, as compared to about $185 a month in the private and public sectors. This wage disparity has led some to speculate incorrectly that this entire sector can be considered to be a labor aristocracy.[23]

After 1914 when the canal was completed, the workers who remained in Panama to maintain the canal and related civilian and military institutions lived in either the one-room tenements in Panama and Colon cities that were owned by the real estate bourgeoisie, or they lived in slightly better quarters under apartheid-like conditions in the Canal Zone. They suffered segregation and exploitation in the American-controlled Canal Zone and racial and ethnic prejudice in Panama proper.[24]

Torrijos, unlike the previous oligarchical administrations, recognized the role of these workers in the struggle against racial discrimination and segregation in the Canal Zone. He "appropriated" that struggle, interpreting and representing it as part of a larger anticolonial effort against the United States.

The Peasantry. The peasants and farmers are the poorest and most exploited class in Panamanian society. They lack good arable land, but more importantly, they lack ownership of the land they work. Historically they depended on the landlord for money and other resources both for producing and marketing their goods.

The land tenure system in Panama is similar to the system prevailing in the rest of Central and South America: while 1 percent of the population owns or controls 34.3 percent of the land, 33 percent of the population owns or controls only 1 percent of the land, many having no more than two hectares of land to cultivate. Clearly, the first group is comprised largely of the landed oligarchy and the second group comprised largely of the peasantry.

The small farmers, who own five to fifty hectares, control 32.8 percent of the land.[25] They usually occupy district and local offices. This is the group that made up the bulk of Torrijos's quasi-legislative National Assembly of Community Representatives.

The medium farmers, those who own or control between 50 and 200 hectares of land, are very closely associated to the landed oligarchy and usually occupy important political positions in the provinces or in the national legislature. They constitute 8.2 percent of the population.

The United States and the Panamanian Military

Overlaid on this class structure and contributing to its crises of political hegemony were the strategic imperatives of the United States. With the building of the canal, Panama became the jugular vein of U.S. hemispheric defense. Although Washington chose not to impose direct colonial rule on the isthmus, as it did over Puerto Rico, it was unwilling to accept prolonged instability there. During the early part of the century, moreover, the American government preferred to use its own forces to control disorder in Panama rather than create an indigenous armed force that might itself threaten U.S. interests.[26] Panama was too vital to risk U.S. dependence on a Somoza or a Batista. Ironically, that reluctance may explain the role ultimately played by Omar Torrijos.

From 1903 to 1936, Panama was a virtual protectorate of the United States. Article III of the Hay-Bunau-Varilla Treaty gave the United States rights as if it were the sovereign government. By Article XXIII, the United States could employ force for the protection and defense of the Panama Railroad and Canal.[27] Article 136 of Panama's 1904 constitution stipulated that the government of the United States guaranteed the independence and sovereignty of Panama, and could intervene anywhere in the country to restore public peace and constitutional order.

And intervene the United States did, twelve times from 1906 to 1928. In many cases, the United States was invited by one or the other parties led by the oligarchy (the liberals and the conservatives).[28] In other cases, the U.S. military came unsolicited. The political effect was to weaken the Panamanian government's claim to legitimacy.

In the wake of the Great Depression and the rise of fascism, adjustments were made in the dependency relationship. The 1936 treaty between Presidents Franklin Roosevelt and Harmodio Arias Madrid abolished the U.S. right of intervention in the affairs of Panama and granted Panamanian businesses some access to Canal Zone markets.[29] Nonetheless, Panama was still obligated to ally with the United States in case of war. Once war came, the government of Panama allowed the United States to establish 130 military sites in Panama, in return for a number of revisions in the U.S. role, none of which altered the basic nature of the relationship. Similar changes were made in the Treaty of Understanding and Mutual Cooperation of 1955: many created new opportunities for Panamanian businessmen in the Canal Zone, but none signalled a restoration of Panamanian sovereignty over the territory.

The status and power of the Panamanian military was derivative of the U.S. relationship with the country. The Panamanian army was abolished in 1904, soon after it attempted a coup d'etat. It was replaced by a paramilitary National Police force, which remained an ineffective and poorly trained institution until the late 1930s. At that time it was reorganized and strengthened under the command of Jose Antonio Remon Cantera. In 1953 Remon transformed the force into a National Guard that combined internal security and defense functions, and had land, sea, and air components. Remon used his position to play the role of presidential king-maker in the post-war years, and himself became president in 1952. Had he not been assassinated under mysterious circumstances two years later, he might well have become a Panamanian Somoza.

Historical Precedents

The crisis of hegemony that resulted in the October Revolution was not the first in Panama's twentieth-century history. Two others preceded it, one during the period 1925-1932 and the second in the period 1947-1952. In both, popular classes were mobilized by middle class groups against the oligarchy and against U.S. colonialism. In both instances, the oligarchy was able, through a variety of means, to restore its control. It was not able, however, to promote economic growth and establish national sovereignty sufficient to secure long-term legitimacy.

The 1925-1932 Crisis. Until the mid-1920s, Panama's civilian leaders were able to maintain their dominance through a mixture of mild anti-Americanism, populism, and periodic U.S. intervention. In the years after World War I, however, there emerged a number of nationalist groups opposed to the oligarchy and the United States. Among them were the General Syndicate of Workers (Sindicato General de Trabajadores), the Communist Group (Grupo Comunista), which represented young Canal Zone workers, the Labor party, the Communist party, the Socialist party, and a middle class civic organization--Community Action (Accion Comunal).

The Tenants League was a special branch of the General Syndicate of Workers. In 1925 it organized tenants in Colon and Panama cities in order to resist a rent hike of 25 to 50 percent imposed by urban landlords, who themselves had just been hit with a new property tax. The government of then-President Rodolfo Chiari created a commission to study the matter and appointed representatives from a government-controlled union (Federacion Obrera de la Republica). The commission approved the rent hike on October 1, and on October 9 the rent strike was called.

Meanwhile, in Panama City, the Tenants League called a demonstration in Santa Plaza for October 10, in violation of a mayoral order suspending all tenants' meetings. The police sought to disperse the demonstration and left several strikers killed and dozens wounded. Yet the number of people in the streets grew, and business was paralyzed.

On October 12 the government of President Rodolfo Chiari invoked Article 136 of the 1904 constitution, which gave the United States the right to intervene to restore peace and order. Chiari called on the U.S. Marines to put down the tenants' strike.[30]

The U.S. military force, under the command of General William Lassiter, remained in Panama from October 12-23. During the course of the occupation, the marines bayoneted to death many Panamanians at Santa Plaza. Many of the strike leaders were deported to Spain (their birthplace). The Tenants League headquarters was closed. In the end, the foreign minister expressed the oligarchy's gratitude to the Americans for a job well done.

The next high tide of political conflict came over the Kellogg-Alfaro Treaty. The pact, negotiated in secrecy, had the effect of locking Panama into a military alliance with the United States. The day before the treaty draft was to be submitted to the National Assembly for ratification, its contents were published in a Mexican newspaper.

Immediately Communal Action, the General Syndicate of Workers, and the newly organized Anti-Imperialist League went into action. Its allies in the Assembly, led by the renowned international lawyer, Harmodio Arias, prevailed upon the body to suspend consideration of the treaty.[31] The Chiari government responded by persecuting, jailing, or exiling radical leaders, and Communal Action went underground.[32]

Communal Action went only one more round with Chiari. The president attempted to impose Florencio Arosemena as his successor, and the popular movement responded by overthrowing the oligarchy's government. Then the United States stepped in. Ambassador Roy Tasco Davis gave the "revolutionaries" an ultimatum to settle the crisis constitutionally by five o'clock that day. By agreement between Communal Action and the oligarchy, Arosemena would appoint Harmodio Arias Madrid as minister of government and justice and then leave the presidency. Arias would be interim chief executive until Ricardo Alfaro, Panama's ambassador in Washington, returned to assume the office.[33] Some of Communal Action's members were co-opted into the government and others were alienated and disillusioned. Those who continued to work on behalf of the popular classes were able to wrest some economic concessions--on the issue of tenants' rights, for example. Fundamentally, however, the oligarchy's rule continued.

The elite's success in splitting Communal Action was in part a function of the movement's internal weaknesses. Its ideology was heavy on anti-Americanism and light on a program to cure Panama's social and economic ills. In addition, Communal Action tried to increase its influence by using racist appeals to sow dissension between the workers of Panama and Colon cities on the one hand, and the black workers of the Canal Zone on the other.

<u>The 1947-1952 Crisis</u>. Panama was relatively quiet through the latter part of the Great Depression and the Second World War. Through an amendment to the 1903 treaty, the Roosevelt administration agreed in 1936 to give up its right on intervention in the affairs of Panama and to grant Panamanian businesses some access to the Canal Zone. When Washington later sought an agreement to link Panama's military fate with that of the United States in case of war, the oligarchy was able to fight off popular opposition. In the context of the fight against fascism, the popular movement lost its will and capacity to challenge the ruling class.

Even so, the oligarchy was too divided to effectively consolidate its hegemony. The most telling manifestation of the elite fragmentation was the presidency of Arnulfo Arias Madrid, which began in 1941. Arias immediately abrogated the 1904 constitution and replaced it with a charter that combined economic interventionism, social progressivism, and political nationalism cum racism. The 1941 constitution called for distribution of public lands to rural families, created a social security system, mandated annual paid vacations, nationalized retail commerce, enfranchised women, and extended legal protection to illegitimate children. The presidential term--that is, the frequency with which that office circulated among the oligarchs--was increased from four to six years. And white racism was elevated to a new level in Panama's social history: in defense of nationality, language, and customs, Caribbean blacks, Chinese, and other undesirable colored aliens were to be excluded or deported.[34]

This ambitious and controversial agenda only alienated the opposition oligarchical parties, and the newly reorganized National Police. The latter removed Arias from power on October 9, 1941. The United States, which had its own reasons to be dissatisfied with the populist president, was not displeased with the outcome.[35] Arias's successor, Adolfo de la Guardia, was a more conventional leader and in return for granting American wartime access to 130 sites in Panama, was able to secure a modest enhancement of Panamanian sovereignty vis-a-vis the United States.[36]

Yet the oligarchy was unprepared for the new challenge posed by the middle and popular classes after the war. On this occasion, the vanguard of the struggle was the Federation of Panamanian Students (FEP), the United Panamanian Teachers, and the Front of Patriotic Youth. Supported by the People's party (i.e., the Communist party, Moscow-oriented) and the Socialist party, these groups in 1944 called for the removal of the de la Guardia government and the election of a Constituent Assembly. After many moves and countermoves, de la Guardia agreed to call an assembly in 1945 empowered to write a new constitution and elect a new president.

In the Constituent Assembly arena, the oligarchy incorporated many social demands made by the middle class, co-opted some middle class leadership, and secured a precarious formula for the continuation of its dominance.[37] As in the 1930s, the middle classes were divided, and they failed to form a political party that would institutionalize their political role. Nonetheless, the middle classes retained the capacity to mobilize the urban masses around social and political issues.

The Filos-Hines treaty, concluded by the U.S. and Panamanian governments in 1947, provided such an issue. The treaty, a product of the emerging Cold War, would have allowed the United States to maintain the 130 military facilities it had obtained for the duration of the war. Student and teacher groups mobilized a nationalist coalition against the agreement. As with the Kellogg-Alfaro treaty, the National Assembly chose not to incur the wrath of the popular classes and declined to ratify the pact.[38] The U.S. military had to evacuate the military sites.

Beaten on a nationalistic issue, the oligarchy was also too divided to put forward sustained presidential leadership. Between 1948 and 1952, there were five presidents, including Arnulfo Arias. Again, Arias attempted to institute radical changes in short order. Again, he alienated key political sectors, particularly the military. Again, he was deposed--on May 10, 1951--in a bloody coup by Colonel Antonio Remon Cantera, head of the National Guard.[39]

Colonel Remon then decided to run for president, instead of continuing the king-maker role that he had played since 1948. He became president in 1952 and took several major steps to stabilize Panamanian politics. He enacted legislation that reduced the number of parties that could compete in national elections (and had the effect of weakening the popular movements). He sought to spur economic growth by instituting an economic policy of protectionism and import substitution. And, to further stimulate economic growth and enhance political legitimacy, Remon successfully concluded the 1955 Treaty of Mutual Understanding and Cooperation with the United States.[40] The treaty opened further the Canal Zone to Panamanian business, and removed some of the slights to Panamanian sovereignty.

Just as the civilian oligarchy was unable in the 1930s to secure political dominance on its own, Remon's death by violence in 1955 shut off the possibility of political hegemony based on an alliance between the military and the oligarchy. In the next crisis, Omar Torrijos would take a very different approach.

NOTES

1. Amos Perlmutter, The Military and Politics in Modern Times (New Haven, 1977), p. x.

2. Ibid., pp. 25-26.

3. Ibid., p. 113.

4. Ibid., p. 26.

5. Ibid., p. 199.

6. M. E. Carranza, Fuerzas Armadas y Estados de Excepcion en America Latina (Mexico, 1978).

7. Bob Jessop, Capitalist State (New York, 1982), p. 148.

8. Leon Trotsky, Russian Revolution, vol. 2 (London, 1965), pp. 155-66. See also Hal Draper, Karl Marx's Theory of Revolution (New York, 1977).

9. Trotsky, Russian Revolution, p. 155.

10. Ibid., p. 157.

11. Ibid., p. 156.

12. Draper, Theory of Revolution, pp. 420-26.

13. Bernardo Sorj, Military Reformism and Social Classes: The Peruvian Experience 1968-1980 (London, 1982), p. 191.

14. Direccion de Estadistica y Censo, Estadisticas Vitales (Panama, 1974).

15. For an analysis of the unequal distribution of urban-rural resources, see Renato Pereira, Panama Fuerzas Armadas y Politica (Panama, 1979), pp. 35-36.

16. See Alfredo Castillero Calvo, Los Negros y Mulatos en Tierra Firme (Panama, 1979).

17. See Velma Newton, The Silver Men: West Indian Labor Migration to Panama: 1850-1914 (Mona, Jamaica, 1984).

18. Ibid., p. 47.

19. See Alfredo Figueroa Navarro, Dominio y Sociedad en el Panama Colombiano: 1831-1903 (Panama, 1978), pp.

342-43. Navarro describes the impact of the black population on the politics of the Liberal party in the 1850s. The migrations also intensified racial conflicts along the transit route, in which the United States was repeatedly involved. See Gerstle Mack, The Land Divided (New York, 1944).

20. Pereira, Panama Fuerzas Armadas, p. 55.

21. For a treatment of the Panamanian economic dominant classes, see an exciting pioneering work by Marco Gandasegui, La Concentracion del Poder Economico en Panama (Panama, 1967).

22. Herbert de Souza, Notes on the Socio-Political Situation in Panama (Toronto, 1975), pp. 4-5.

23. See Pereira, Panama Fuerzas Armadas, pp. 70-77.

24. See George Westerman, The Problem of West Indian Off-Spring in Panama: A Study of the Relationship of Ethnic and Cultural Groups in a Cosmopolitan Setting (Panama, 1944); George Westerman, Urban Housing in Panama (Panama, 1955); George Westerman, The West Indian Worker in the Canal Zone (National Civic League, 1951); George Priestley and Gerardo Maloney, "El Grupo Antillano en el Proceso Politico Panameno," Tareas, no. 33 (September-November 1975), pp. 11-27.

25. These figures are adopted from Marco Gandasegui, El Campesinado Panameno (Panama, 1980).

26. See Ramiro Guerra, La Expansion Territorial de los Estados Unidos (Editorial de las Ciencias Sociales, La Habana, 1975), pp. 385-86; and Gustavo Mellander, The United States in Panamanian Politics (Danville, Ill., 1971), p. 31 and p. 66.

27. See the Hay-Bunau-Varilla Treaty in Annex I of Panama y Los Estados Unidos de America ante el Problema del Canal (Panama, 1966), p. 444. Samuel Bemis, Latin American Policy in the United States (New York, 1943), p. 105 argues that Article XXXV of the treaty contained words momentous for U.S.-Latin American diplomacy. This article gave the United States the right to guarantee the neutrality of the isthmus and free transit from one sea to the other, and the right to guarantee the sovereignty of the territory. Within the context of U.S. expansion into California and the Mexican territorial cession of 1848, the treaty was important for the United States. For a Panamanian interpretation of Article XXXV, see Mario Rijfkogel, "Sobre el Articulo XXV del Tratado Mallarino-Bidlack," Relaciones entre Panama y los Estados

Unidos (Panama, 1974). For a good historical synthesis of U.S. canal diplomacy in the nineteenth century, see Julio Yau, El Canal de Panama: Calvario de un Pueblo (Madrid, 1972), especially pp. 31-37.

28. Mellander, Panamanian Politics, p. x.

29. Alberto Quiros Guardia argues that the only ones to oppose the 1936 treaty were members of the National Defense League, dissidents of Communal Action. See his "Lucha Por la Soberania" (unpublished manuscript, Panama, n.d.), pp. 31-32.

30. For a complete treatment of the 1925 rent strike, see Alexander Cuevas, El Movimiento Inquilinario de 1925 (Panama, 1975).

31. Celestino Andres Arauz, C.M. Gasteozoro, and Armando Munoz, La Historia de Panama en sus Textos, vol. 2 (Panama, 1979), p. 134.

32. Interview with Roberto Clement, founding member of Communal Action, Panama, July 1973.

33. J. Conte Porras, Arnulfo Arias Madrid (Panama, 1980), pp. 75-76.

34. See Title II, Article 23, Paragraph 3 and Title II, Articles 12-22 of the 1941 Constitution of the Republic of Panama.

35. For a full discussion of U.S.-Panama relations during World War II, see John Andrew Cooley, "The United States and the Panama Canal, 1938-1947. Policy Formulation and Implementation from Munich Through the Early Years of the Cold War" (Ph.D. diss., Ohio State University, 1972).

36. In return Washington agreed to honor Panama's request contained in Arnulfo's twelve-point petition. This petition requested, among other things, that the United States transfer to Panama all hydraulic works in the cities of Colon and Panama; that the United States return all Panama Railroad lots in Panama and Colon cities; that the United States cooperate to stamp out contraband articles coming from the Canal Zone into the Republic of Panama; that the United States construct a tunnel or bridge to unite and permit travel from Panama City to the hinterland (the canal had divided the country in two halves); that the United States grant to Panama jurisdiction over all roads and highways constructed by the United States in Panama; and that the United States guarantee work on the Canal Zone for all Panamanians or

immigrants permitted under Panamanian laws. This last point was in reference to Caribbean workers whose numbers had reached, by 1942, 32,565. This figure was only higher in 1913 when the numbers had reached 44,711 employees.

37. Selma Noriega de Jurado, Verdad y Miseria de Nuestros Partidos Politicos (Panama, 1978), p. 5.

38. For a detailed account of the Filos-Hines issue, see J. Conte Porras, La Rebelion de las Esfinjes: Historia del Movimiento Estudiantil Panameno (Panama, 1978), pp. 101-78.

39. For various and diverse interpretations of the events surrounding this coup, see Larry Pippin, The Remon Era (Stanford, 1964); J. Conte Porras, La Rebelion; Alesandro Russo Berguido, Horario de una Traicion: 10 de Mayo de 1951 (Panama, 1961).

40. For a political analysis of the 1955 treaty, see Humberto E. Ricord, "El Tratado Remon-Eisenhower," Relaciones Entre Panama y los Estados Unidos (Panama, 1974), pp. 252-64.

2

The 1960s Crisis of Hegemony and the Emergence of the Torrijos Regime

This chapter describes (a) the conditions that led to the takeover of power by the National Guard in 1968; (b) the steps taken by the Guard to consolidate its rule, with respect both to internal struggles for power and relationships with key political groups; (c) the Torrijos regime's approach to macroeconomic policy as a solution to economic growth in Panama; and (d) the regime's foreign policy, with particular attention to the canal issue. The remainder of the study will examine Torrijos's actions with respect to the other central item on the Panamanian political agenda--the building of stable and mass-based political institutions.

The Collapse of the Civilian Oligarchy

In the 1960s four developments brought about a crisis of hegemony that culminated in the revolution of October 1968. First of all, economic growth in the 1960s, based on a policy of import substitution, did not bring quick benefits to the majority of the Panamanian people. Second, the popular movement was again radicalized in response to the economic situation: workers and the urban masses mounted a struggle for employment and a $0.40 minimum wage. Third, the middle class, led by student organizations, stepped up the struggle for sovereignty over the Canal Zone. Lastly, the oligarchy's inability to institute needed reforms or to secure the decolonization of the Canal Zone caused it to be seriously split. In October 1968 the National Guard stepped into the breach.

The Economic Crisis. On the surface, Panama's economy performed well during the decade of the 1960s. The GNP doubled in that time, from $415.8 million in 1960 to over $897 million in 1970. Exports of goods and services tripled during that period, and the sale of goods increased by 12.9 percent from 1961 to 1970.[1] As a share of total manufacturing, light industry (clothing, food, beverages, etc.) had dropped from 70 percent in 1960 to 59.6 percent in 1968.[2] Julio Manduley summarized the structural transformation:

> This rapid expansion made it possible to finance higher import levels, accelerating capital formation and the development of industry. . . . Industry was experiencing what for local purposes we can consider as the second, and last, phase of import substitution. Foreign capital made sure that there were openings still available in the range of industrial goods (chemicals, rubber, plastics, and petroleum). In 1968, eighteen of twenty-two foreign firms with direct investments in the industrial sector had initiated operations during the decade. . . . By the end of the decade, the import-substitution process seemed to have come to a definitive halt; the participation of national production in the total supply of manufactures reached 35 percent in 1968, having been 32 percent in 1961.[3]

But economic growth had its negative side as well. On the one hand, the imports of equipment and machinery had to be paid for. The export of services to the Canal Zone did not play its historic role of offsetting deficits in the balance of payments. Increasingly, the shortfalls were met by direct and indirect foreign investment, U.S. government loans, and foreign bank loans.[4] Even increased U.S. economic assistance, which annually averaged around $14 million in the Kennedy administration and $13 million in the Johnson administration, had little impact.[5]

Nor did the economic aid and economic growth rectify the inequitable distribution of wealth and income. Panama remained a country beset by hunger, malnutrition, disease, unemployment, and underemployment. An Alliance for Progress report of 1973 drew a grim picture of the mid-sixties crisis:

--per capita income was $531, but 5 percent of the population received more than one-third of the income.

--half of those employed were farmers, and the great majority of farmers earned less than $100 per year.

--the country spent $12 million in 1968 to import staples, even though it had the potential to be a food exporter. Lack of transportation in the interior, inequitable land holdings, archaic agricultural methods, and the educational system were to blame.

--population was growing at an incredible 3.3 percent annually and by over 4 percent in the urban areas, where the jobless congregated in already over-crowded slums.

--by 1966 unemployment reached 25 percent. The largest employers were the government (30,000 employees), the Canal Zone (13,000), and the United Fruit Company (11,000).

--whereas Panama possessed over 2,000 manufacturing firms, only sixty employed fifty or more laborers, and these sixty (accounting for 61 percent of the nation's manufactures by value) were owned almost entirely by members of the oligarchy or foreign firms.[6]

The regional disparities, which had not changed since the nineteenth century, affected mostly the rural dispossessed and the urban unemployed. Of the $894.5 million GNP for 1970, 82 percent is accounted for by the commercial and industrial sectors concentrated in Panama and Colon cities. The rural areas, where 52 percent of the work force was located, accounted for a mere 10 percent. Rural per capita income was approximately $43.84 per year.[7]

<u>The Rebirth of the Popular Movement</u>. The structural limitations of the industrialization process and its failure to benefit large sectors of the population set off a series of protests from urban groups.

As the decade began, workers, students, and the urban unemployed organized to protest hunger and high rents, and to struggle for a forty-cent-per-hour minimum wage. A number of demonstrations, rent strikes, and labor strikes were held in support of these goals. The bourgeoisie, which in 1960 paid wages of twenty-five cents an hour, vehemently opposed the minimum wage movement.

In addition, there were repeated strikes by urban transport workers, public school teachers, and banana workers. The liberal governments of Presidents Roberto Chiari (1960-64) and Marco Robles (1964-68) went through the motions of Alliance for Progress reforms, but tended to rely on severe repression to deal with the working class movement, especially the banana workers union.[8]

Nonetheless, the forty-cent minimum wage was achieved. The banana workers continued organizing. And industrialization spurred the growth of the working class, and therefore of the labor movement.

It is within this context of economic growth and mass political discontent that on January 9, 1964, over 200 students of the National Institute marched across the boundary from Panama into the Canal Zone to demand that the Panamanian flag fly beside that of the United States as agreed to earlier by Presidents Roberto Chiari and John Kennedy.

The Panamanian students' demand was met with hostility by Canal Zone students who refused to allow Panama's flag to fly beside that of the United States. When Panamanian students insisted, a fight broke out, leading Canal Zone authorities to intervene and to call on the U.S. military to restore order. When the dust settled, three U.S. servicemen and twenty-two Panamanians had died.

President Chiari broke diplomatic relations with the United States, threatened to take the issue to the United Nations, but later agreed to allow the International Commission of Jurists to investigate. The Commission blamed both sides, and "indicted the American police and military for the degree of force employed to restrain the rioters."[9] By April 3, 1964, Panama and the United States had restored diplomatic relations and had agreed to discuss or negotiate a new treaty. The diplomatic crisis was over, but the quest for real sovereignty remained a thorny issue in U.S.-Panamanian relations.

<u>The Abortive Canal Treaty</u>. In June of 1967 Presidents Lyndon Johnson and Marco Robles announced agreement on a common approach to a new treaty governing the canal. The two governments proposed to negotiate a new treaty to replace the pact of 1903; conclude an agreement to legitimize all U.S. military bases in Panama; and reach an agreement over the construction of a sea-level canal. In return, the United States would recognize Panama's right to exercise sovereignty over the existing canal, to recover jurisdiction over the Zone, and to receive a larger annuity. A new U.S.-Panama partnership would assume from the Panama Canal Company authority for defense, neutrality, and operation of the existing canal and any that might be built.

The Panamanian Students Federation (FEP) led the fight against the Robles-Johnson treaty proposals. The FEP had been steeled by its leadership of the struggle with the United States in 1964, and the memory of the mysterious assassination of one of its young leaders was still fresh. As in 1926 and 1947, the popular movement successfully exerted pressure on the National Assembly to reject the treaty proposals.[10]

The Oligarchy Splits. The oligarchy found itself unable to cope with the forces undermining its rule. As in the past, the renascent popular movement and the strife over the canal increased the demands on the regime. Complicating matters was the fact that the oligarchy was deeply split over economic policy.

At issue was the strategy of import substitution. The commercial bourgeoisie resented the high tariffs that protected the manufacturing sector, especially in food, clothing, and footwear. When the rate of industrialization slowed, the commercial groups were quick to suggest alternative developmental policies. Even more approaches surfaced as the various industrial, commercial, and financial groups discussed whether or not Panama should join the Central American Common Market.[11]

For the first time, the National Confederation of Private Enterprise (CONEP), a political organization of business groups, was split down the middle. The Chamber of Commerce, representing commercial enterprises, was opposed to joining the regional common market. It proposed instead that Panama convert its entire economy into a free trade zone, a la Hong Kong, with no duties or quotas.[12] The Industrial Syndicate, supported by the AID-sponsored Industrial Development Corporation, opposed the end of protection and favored a gradual integration into the common market.

With the oligarchy so deeply divided, the 1968 political campaign was unusually bitter. The contest pitted President Robles against Arnulfo Arias, the long-time bete-noire of the National Guard. Symptomatic of the seriousness of the hegemony crisis, Arias got the support of many leading industrialists, and secured the defection to his side of Roberto Chiari, Robles's predecessor. Yet for tactical reasons, Arias initially sought to avoid alienating the National Guard, which had deposed him twice before, and the United States, the usual target of his nationalistic rhetoric.

The pro-Arias forces in the National Assembly were able to secure the impeachment of Robles on grounds that he had tampered with election procedures and named First Vice President Max Delvalle to replace him. The National Guard read this move as an effort to guarantee Arias's election, and so threw its support to Robles. Arias then began to attack the Guard publicly. In return, the Guard ransacked Arias's headquarters and jailed many of his sympathizers.

On May 12 Arias won the presidency for the third time and took office on October 1. Ten days later rumors circulated that he was about to reshuffle the hierarchy of the National Guard. The same day, the Guard removed him from office. A figurehead military-civilian junta was installed; the civilian members came from or were associated with the oligarchy. Colonels Omar Torrijos and Boris Martinez held real power.

The Consolidation of Power and the Rise of Torrijos

The immediate reaction to the coup was negative. On October 14 the administrative board of the National University of Panama issued a manifesto to the nation denouncing the takeover and calling for a speedy return to civilian government. The manifesto was signed by all members of the board, students, faculty members, deans, and the rector.[13] It thus reflected the opinion of the critical student and teacher groups.

At around the same time, an organization reflecting opinion of the politicized masses sounded a similar note. The Movement of National Unification, Development, and Guidance (MUNDO), which was the most influential civic and political organization in the large (80,000 residents) militant shantytown of San Miguelito, issued a position paper entitled "The Fourth Line." The communique took a "pox-on-all-your-houses" approach, condemning Arias, Liberal party leader Samudio, and the military. Of the latter it said, "We do not want to be subordinated to the military. We will not accept tyranny in any form, for tyrannies are the detractors of our liberty and progress."[14]

In response, the National Guard began by attacking obvious abuses and dealing with putative threats to national stability (what Jose Nun calls "moralizing"[15]). By November 1 more than fifteen National Guard officers had received dishonorable discharges. On November 2, the Guard cracked down on the most prominent "numbers-men" operating in the popular communities, who the regime claimed were robbing the national treasury of much needed funds by drawing business away from the National Lottery System. On November 3 forty members of the Party of the People (the Communist party) were arrested and jailed. At the same time, the regime conducted search-and-destroy missions against other so-called leftist groups operating on the Panama-Costa Rica border.

In December the National Guard moved against the University, the base for the student movement. On the fifth, the government closed down and occupied the campus, ostensibly because of some violence between students over a disputed election for rector. The real reason was that many university groups had begun to agitate against the military regime. To justify its action the Guard claimed it found a large cache of arms, rifles, shotguns, molotovs, acids, and communist literature.[16] On December 17 Roger Decerega, who would later occupy many positions in the Torrijos regime, assumed administrative control of the university, governing with a board of regents composed of citizens appointed from both the public and private sectors.

Another target was the political institutions of the oligarchy. In October the military closed the National Assembly and proscribed all political parties. To add insult to injury, Colonel Boris Martinez, one of the two strongmen, jailed many members of the oligarchy for embezzlement of public funds. Not wishing to be regarded as pawns of the military, five civilian members of the junta who were close to the oligarchy resigned on January 8, 1969.[17]

In reality, the National Guard was split into three distinct groups over what to do with the power that had been seized. One, represented by Colonel Boris Martinez, the leader of the coup, favored a strictly authoritarian regime. Another, represented by Colonels Ramiro Silvera and Amado Sanjur, proposed a passive approach to the crisis of hegemony by returning power to the civilians, in the person of David Samudio, Robles's ally in the Liberal party. The third group, led by Colonel Omar Torrijos, advocated a military regime supported by popular groups, similar to the Velasco regime in Peru.

Which approach to take was decided through struggles for power within the military command. Martinez was the first to go, exiled to Miami in February 1969. Nine months later, while Torrijos was visiting Mexico, Sanjur and Silvera and others led a coup against him. With the connivance of an ally, Major Manuel Noriega, Torrijos returned immediately to Panama and put down the coup.[18] He reorganized the general staff of the National Guard and entered 1970 as its undisputed leader.

Torrijos next moved to get the middle sectors on the regime's side. He had witnessed how the student and professional organizations could bring down a regime. Key among them was the FEP, which was the youth section of the Communist Party of the People and which in 1967 had led the fight against the Robles-Johnson treaty proposals. Torrijos secured a pledge from the FEP of its unconditional and ardent support of the regime by awarding it control of the newly reopened university and by granting some of its key members important ministerial and subministerial positions.[19]

The student movement would soon split over the issue of unconditional support. Beginning in 1972, new independent leftist groups emerged, such as the Federation of Revolutionary Students (based in the National Institute), the Guaycucho-NIR and the Circulo Camilo Torres (both based in the Law Faculty of the University of Panama). In November 1974 the Party of the People split with the FEP: both organizations lost members as a result, and the "new-left" student organizations were able to make significant gains. But those groups never mounted a serious challenge to the Torrijos regime, for most lacked political experience, organizational resources, and theoretical clarity. Torrijos's strategy of co-optation had worked.

A Shift in Macroeconomic Policy

As will be described in detail in later chapters, Torrijos sought to build institutions that would involve the popular classes in politics for the first time. But he knew that the legitimacy of his regime could only be permanently established if those openings of participation were accompanied by an economic program that would create opportunities for all Panamanians and job security for labor. To that end, he approved a progressive labor code in 1972 and attempted thereby to organize and unify the labor movement under the umbrella of the military. That strategy evolved over time, and came to encompass the following elements:

--enhancing Panama's role as a transport hub and building it up as a financial center, a "platform for transnational services."[20]

--in the production sector, abandoning the policy of import substitution through protectionism, and giving new stimulus to exports, particularly agricultural exports.

Each of these initiatives would require substantial government spending to build the necessary infrastructure. But the regime chose not to displace the private sector, a course of action which, if taken, might have united the oligarchy against the military. As it was, key sectors of the bourgeoisie linked to international capital, such as the group of Modernizing Entrepreneurs, saw the possibilities for rapid accumulation through expanding the export of goods and services, and they cooperated with the regime. Many small- and medium-sized industrial concerns that had benefited from protectionist policies objected to the new policies, as did the commercial and landowning oligarchy. But they did not have the power to block the initiatives.

The first component of the economic program to be implemented was in the area of finance. As early as 1969, Torrijos told a group of U.S. businessmen that he would pursue "a policy of expanding markets and ample maritime, aeronautical, banking, legal, and labor facilities, and a cultural attitude favorable to international business." He promised "an honest, modern and more responsible public administration."[21] To a New York business audience, he said, "We have a government team which is young, professional and competent. . . . There is a stability and calm in our country today, and we are functioning in an orderly fashion."[22] (Panama had added attractions because of the fourteen U.S. military bases, excellent communication systems, and use of the U.S. dollar as the currency.)

In the wake of that speech, Torrijos passed the 1970 Banking Reform, which allowed, among other things, the unrestricted movement of money in and out of the country. In July 1970 an International Financial Center was established with a Banking Center at its core.[23] By December 1976 the number of banks with branches in Panama would increase to seventy-six (in 1960 there were only five) and their deposits would total $11.3 billion (compared to $341 million in foreign bank deposits in 1968).

Aside from banking reform, the other early economic policy emphasis of the regime was to foster redistribution through public spending, public sector employment, acquisition of private and public lands for agricultural reform, and social services.[24] Expenditures in these areas were as important for the legitimation of the regime as they were for developing the national economy. In the area of health, for example, the government created 800 local community health groups (*comites de salud*), designed to involve the urban and particularly rural communities in the organization, delivery, and maintenance of health care. Before the promulgation of the 1972 constitution, the health groups were the closest thing to a structure of local participation.

By the early 1970s it became clear, however, that a policy of redistribution was limiting the prospects for economic growth. An Alliance for Progress report on Panama declared: "The experience of 1971-72 suggests that a conflict has appeared between the policy of economic incentives for production and the policy which seeks to redistribute income through structural change."[25] The report recommended that "it must be determined which of the objectives can temporarily be given lesser priority so that an optimal path of action is achieved through time within the potential availabilities of finance and human resources."[26] As a result of the re-evaluation of policy, the percentage of the government spending on social services declined.

The architect of the new policy was Nicolas Ardito Barletta, an economist trained at the University of Chicago and head of the Ministry of Planning and Economic Policy, which was created in 1973. One prong of Barletta's policy was to energize the agricultural sector as a way of addressing the problems of poverty, unemployment, food supply, urban slums, and inadequate exports. Among the projects envisaged were government ownership of sugar refineries; sectoralization of agricultural lands to increase production of basic grains for domestic consumption; and promotion of agribusiness. A number of commodities were slated for export markets: shrimp, coffee, cacao, melons, pineapples, citrus fruits, flowers, tobacco, and cattle derivatives.

The second prong of Barletta's policy was to broaden Panama's role as a communications and financial center beyond the point reached by Torrijos's banking reforms. As indicated in a 1974 interview,[27] Barletta had a long agenda of projects, for which he hoped to attract private capital:

--a new international airport at Tocumen.

--expansion of the Colon Free Zone.

--construction of an oleduct running north-south along the canal.

--construction of container ports on both sides of the canal.

--construction of an international convention center.

--encouragement of tourism.

--urban renewal of Panama City to make it fit for its new role.

Foreign Policy

Politically speaking, Omar Torrijos could not have pursued an open-minded international economic policy designed to make Panama a more integral part of the world economy had he not simultaneously taken an unmistakably nationalistic, anti-American posture in foreign policy.

Torrijos's approach to the canal dispute was clearly reflected in a speech to over 200,000 Panamanians on October 11, 1971, the third anniversary of the coup. To the assembly of 200,000 Panamanians Torrijos said, "...Gentlemen, we also want to talk about a problem that's in all of our hearts, that is, the problem of our relations with the canal zone. We want to talk about that problem, a problem that Omar Torrijos and the Panamanian people see as essentially a sentimental problem." He continued, "Allow our workers and our ambassadors from friendly republics who are present today to ask what country or people in the world supports the humiliation of a foreign flag nailed in its heart?" He warned, "We are reaching the limits of our patience," and reiterated the challenge to foreign correspondents. "Let the foreign correspondents ask what country or people of the Americas or of the world supports the presence of a foreign governor contiguous to its own territory? By what right? Governor of what?"[28]

Torrijos kept up the pressure on the United States. In March 1973, for example, he was able to use a United Nations Security Council meeting in Panama to embarrass the United States, getting the support of all the nations present for his denunciation of the United States. Eleven months later, the two countries reached an eight-point agreement on the principles that should underlie a new treaty. Leftist groups questioned some of the points, including those of joint military defense, legalization of U.S. military bases, and U.S. rights regarding any sea-level canal. Torrijos, however, was able to draw on his regime's image as "anti-imperialist" and "socialist" to ward off the criticisms.

Part of that image had been created by a general shift toward a more independent foreign policy. Torrijos established relations with several countries in the socialist bloc, such as Bulgaria, Rumania, Poland, Czechoslovakia, the German Democratic Republic, Hungary, and Yugoslavia. The regime also opened embassies in several African and Middle Eastern countries. In August 1974 Panama defied a U.S. blockade and established diplomatic relations with Cuba.[29] One year later Panama joined the nonaligned movement.

Thus demonstrating that he was not "Washington's boy," Torrijos was able, to an extent not possible by his predecessors, to defuse the canal as an internal political issue. His nationalistic, confrontational style vis-a-vis the Americans gave his regime a store of legitimacy that he drew upon in facing the other political challenge--the building of political institutions designed to make crises of hegemony a thing of the past.

NOTES

1. Julio Manduley, "Panama: Notes on the Structure, Current Situation and Perspectives" (Unpublished manuscript, Panama, circa 1976), p. 10.

2. See Direccion General de Planificacion y Administracion, Departamento de Planificacion, Estudios Sectoriales: Diagnostico Sector Industrial (Panama, November 1971), p. 11.

3. Manduley, "Panama: Notes on the Structure," pp. 10-11.

4. Estudios Sectoriales, p. 52.

5. Walter LaFeber, The Panama Canal: Crisis in Historical Perspective (New York, 1978), p. 133.

6. Alliance for Progress Report of 1973, as quoted in LaFeber, The Panama Canal, pp. 150-51.

7. Estudios Sectoriales, pp. 30-31.

8. For a detailed analysis of the banana workers' attempt at organizing, repression by the oligarchical state, and workers' resistance, see Cesar Pereira Burgos, "Experiencias y Signigicacion del Movimiento de Trabajadores Bananeros de Bocas Del Toro," Tareas, no. 4 (1961), pp. 26-44. For a more comprehensive treatment of United Fruit's impact on Panama's society and politics, see Humberto Ricord, et al., Panama y la Frutera: Una Batalla Contra el Colonialismo (Panama, 1974). And for a detailed analysis of the 1960s, see Cinco Ensayos (Panama, circa 1968), which covers Panama's politics from 1942 to 1962. Its essays are important in that they document the ambivalent role of the middle sectors, the decline of the traditional power of the oligarchy, and the rise of the military.

9. Lester D. Langley, The United States and the Caribbean in the Twentieth Century (Athens, 1985), p. 247.

10. The politics of the 1967 treaty proposals is treated in LaFeber, The Panama Canal, pp. 145-48.

11. Charles Denton, "Interest Groups in Panama and Central American Common Market," Interamerican Economic Affairs 21 (1967):49-60.

12. Ibid., p. 56.

13. Administrative Board of the University of Panama, "Manifiesto a La Nacion" (Panama, October 14, 1968).

14. Movimiento de Unificacion Nacional de Desarrollo y Orientacion, "Hacia Una Reestructuracion del Pais: Comunicado de la Cuarta Linea" (circa 1968), p. 1.

15. Jose Nun, "A Latin American Phenomenon--The Middle Class Military Coup," in James Petras and Maurice Zeitlin, eds., <u>Latin America: Reform or Revolution</u> (New York, 1968), pp. 180-81.

16. See <u>Star & Herald</u>, December 5, 1968; and Aristides Royo, "New Structures of Participation" (Lecture delivered at the University of Panama on March 25, 1974).

17. In a letter addressed to Colonel Jose M. Pinilla Fabrega, president of the provisional junta, and to Colonel Bolivar Urrutia Parilla, member of the provisional junta, the following cabinet members resigned: Eduardo Morgan, minister of government and justice; Carlos Alfredo Lopez Guevara, minister of foreign relations; Henry Ford, minister of finance; Celso Carbonnel, minister of public works; and Rafael Zubieta, minister of agriculture, commerce, and industry. The letter stated, "When we accepted our present positions, we thought we would be part of a revolutionary and Christian government in which the military would attend to security matters and the government, made up exclusively of civilians, would attend to all other matters of State. Much to our dismay, there is no coordination between the civilian cabinet members and the military since the latter has made economic and civil rights decisions without first consulting with the civilian cabinet." All Panamanian dailies carried the text of this letter on January 9, 1969.

18. The entire story is told from a position sympathetic to Torrijos in Medoro Lagos and Otelio Miranda, <u>El General Volvio: 15 de Diciembre de 1969</u> (Panama, 1970).

19. Most notable are the cases of Adolfo Ahumada, commissioner of the National Legislative Commission and later minister of labor and minister of government; and Eligio Salas, commissioner of the National Legislative Commission and later chancellor of the University of Panama.

20. This term was coined by Xabier Gorostiaga in "Las Inversiones Extranjeras en Panama: Su Impacto en la Estructura Economica del Pais," in Rafael Menjivar, ed.,

La Inversion Extranjera en Centroamerica (San Jose, Costa Rica, 1974), pp. 324-25.

21. Omar Torrijos, *La Batalla de Panama* (Buenos Aires, 1973), p. 29.

22. Ibid., p. 34.

23. The International Financial Center also included a Reinsurance Center to insure the goods produced in the Colon Free Zone, and, after 1975, the Latin American Export Bank.

24. *United Nations Statistical Abstract* (1969), p. 217.

25. Organization of American States, Inter-American Committee on the Alliance for Progress, "Domestic Efforts and the Needs for External Financing for the Development of Panama" (unpublished manuscript, August 1973), p. 102.

26. Ibid., p. 56.

27. These views were outlined in an interview with Ricardo Lince and published in *El Tecniquito, Boletin Informativo del Ministerio de Planificacion y Politica Economica* 2, no. 19 (Panama, 1974).

28. Torrijos, *La Batalla de Panama*, pp. 83-92. [author's translation]

29. *Star & Herald*, August 20 and August 25, 1974.

3

Demobilization and Incorporation of a Shanty Community: The Case of San Miguelito

San Miguelito lies northeast of Panama City, and in 1968 this shanty community had over 68,000 residents who had migrated from every district of the nine provinces of the Republic.[1] The many social and economic needs resulting from rapid growth were of great concern to political as well as religious leaders. And in the 1960s the Catholic church established various programs in the community.

The San Miguelito experiment resulted from the negative reaction of San Miguelito religious and lay leaders to the military coup. San Miguelito leadership quickly mobilized the community to oppose what they called dictatorship and to support democracy.

The military on the other hand, realizing the scope of the political problem as well as the economic plight of San Miguelito, responded by proposing talks with community leaders.

As a result of these talks, a special district was created and given the status of an autonomous municipality. Administratively, this meant that the community was no longer subordinated to the municipality of Panama City; economically, it meant that the new municipality would be able to regulate itself in the areas of planning and fiscal policy; and politically, it meant greater and more direct participation by the people of San Miguelito. This was the formula of local popular participation on which Torrijos built the National Assembly of Community Representatives: local administration, economic initiative, and direct political participation.

San Miguelito in Historical Perspective

San Miguelito, the largest and most popular of several shanty communities, began to grow during World

War II. During the war period, many people from the interior provinces were attracted by job opportunities resulting from substantial U.S. investment in the transit zone.

Although some of those who came to the cities of Panama returned to their rural communities after the war, many remained and sent for relatives to join them. However, as the rural-to-urban migrations continued even after the war, the traditional slum tenements of Maranon, Calidonia, Chorrillo, and San Miguel all became overcrowded and, as a result, more expensive. So, many of the new immigrants began to settle on the hilly lands along the Trans-Isthmian Highway, that is, in San Miguelito.[2] These lands were held by a few wealthy Panamanian real estate speculators and foreign firms.[3]

San Miguelito consisted of 32,000 hectares that were divided into eight large farms (fincas).[4] And although the slum community occupied only 4,500 hectares, there were increasing conflicts between landlords and squatters over the use of the land. As the population grew in the 1950s, landlords responded by burning and destroying the makeshift shacks. The squatters responded by organizing, not only for protection, but to pressure the government for public services, such as light and water. One such organization was the Civic Society of Farmers and Dwellers of San Miguelito. This organization grew out of the struggles against Compania de Tierras de Monto Oscuro, S.A., whose owner Jose Narciso Recuero was forced to sell the company's 600 hectares to the national government.[5]

Several of the landlords appealed to the national government for a solution to the San Miguelito problems. The response of President Ernesto de la Guardia, through the passage of Law 17 of 1958, was the creation of the Housing and Urbanization Institute (IVU).[6]

The IVU had as its main function the management and control of San Miguelito. But rather than develop a comprehensive plan to solve the squatters' problems, the IVU approached the situation piecemeal.

It worked with the Civic Society in settling land problems and in setting up government housing programs. The programs were basically of two types: self-help and "own effort." In the first category, the IVU gave land and materials to the squatters, who built each house with the help of twenty others. These houses were then raffled. In the second program, the squatters paid for the labor and materials with joint loans from IVU and the Inter-American Development Bank. The interest on these loans was as low as 3 percent. Basically, this type of housing responded to the needs of those squatters who at least had jobs. Those in the first category did not. The IVU also began the removal of urban slum dwellers from the Maranon sector of Panama City (which was quickly becoming the most expensive real estate property in Panama) to the land in San Miguelito purchased by the government. The government's failure to provide social services to the San Miguelito slum made it ripe for politicization, and the agent of that process was the church.

The Chicago Priests

In 1963 the Catholic church urged Father Leo T. Mahon and two other priests to establish an experimental parish in San Miguelito. Father Mahon had worked extensively in Chicago's Mexican and Puerto Rican communities setting up consciousness-building programs (*concientizacion*). He arrived in Panama in 1963 to set up a similar program in San Miguelito.[7]

He immediately elaborated a document called the "San Miguelito Paper," which was signed by the priests of San Miguelito.[8] The document outlined much of the philosophy and objectives of the Chicago group. The principal task was to create a "family," that is, a Christian community. Other tasks were to form social rather than individual consciousness and to form a community that would fulfill the law, and not merely observe it.[9] In order to achieve these goals, a select task force of trained and committed priests would assist and serve as a catalyst for change. These priests would act as co-creators, thought-provokers, revolutionaries, and brothers, not merely as teachers, modernizers, administrators, or fathers.

Father Mahon set up a *concientizacion* program to test his approach. Through a set of informal meetings with select community families, the program essentially emphasized the socioeconomic conditions in the area. These discussion groups were later limited to select men in the area. In the sessions, the role of the saints was de-emphasized because, according to one church organizer, "This was a mere image of the traditional political system, where you offer a couple of pesos to someone with 'palanca' or 'pull,' and he fixes your license for you. People would burn candles to the Saints and feel no responsibility for themselves; they thought the Saints would straighten out their problems for them."[10]

In essence, then, the church organizers were organizing the San Miguelito residents to oppose entering into the traditional clientele system.[11] But in many respects, because of his role as father, organizer, administrator, or teacher, Father Mahon made all important decisions in San Miguelito.

The second phase of the informal sessions held by Mahon and the Chicago priests in 1967 were called <u>cursillos de iniciacion</u>. These sessions were meant to strengthen the nuclear family and as such were limited to married couples. In the <u>cursillos</u>, discussions were led by laymen on such topics as "Christ as a revolutionary," the true meaning of the sacraments, and the nature of the Christian ideal. There was always a concluding discussion on the need for action on the part of the laymen. The participants of these sessions formed what became MUNDO--Movement of National Unification, Development, and Guidance.[12]

Ramon Hernandez of MUNDO characterized the organization as one that believed in a "new politics." The emphasis of this "new politics" was man. He said that man can make politics good as well as bad. All that was needed was to instill in man a Christian spirit.[13]

MUNDO's task was therefore political, that is, to continue the <u>concientizacion</u> program in order to prepare the members of the San Miguelito population to arrive at intelligent, sensible, and democratic decisions. Hernandez said that they eliminated the option of actually forming a political party because of money and the political unpreparedness of MUNDO's membership to focus on national issues.[14]

<u>Structure and Finance of MUNDO</u>

Organizationally, MUNDO was first structured by calling a general meeting to select representatives from each of nine sectors. The representatives were charged with political-civic organizing and with working with government agencies such as IVU, training and sensitizing IVU personnel to the needs of San Miguelito residents. Representatives were required to work full time, and financing was obtained from three sources: private business firms, IVU and the Agency for International Development (AID).[15] Although it is not clear how AID monies reached MUNDO, we know that AID sponsored and controlled a Community Development Agency that operated as a program out of the Ministry of Labor and Welfare.[16] MUNDO was closely linked to this agency.

Although Father Mahon worked closely with MUNDO, it was no longer dependent on the Chicago priests. It now became increasingly dependent on private enterprise and on AID funds. As Eric De Leon noted, if one day these "godfathers" said no to MUNDO's financial needs, the organization would be asphyxiated.[17]

MUNDO showed signs of political division during the 1968 presidential elections. The politicians inundated San Miguelito in search of bloc votes. Hernandez later reflected, "Since we represented leadership in the community, both sides tried to use us. They offered to give us certain things if the people voted for them. When we refused to go along, the politicians withdrew all their financial support and we found ourselves without enough money to continue our work. So in order to sustain our families, we tooks jobs with the Church (San Miguelito parish) or sought work somewhere else."[18] The situation was critical, for at this time AID money was also quickly drying up. This, in short, was the situation of the San Miguelito community prior to the coup of 1968.

Reaction of San Miguelito to the Coup

As noted in Chapter 2, the organized sectors of MUNDO and their constituents were the ones who openly opposed the military coup of October 11, 1968. At first, said Hernandez, MUNDO's position was misrepresented in the press, which viewed San Miguelito as pawns of the recently deposed oligarchy. However, after several demonstrations, some as large as 6,000 people, Colonel Torrijos appointed Juan Materno Vasquez and Dr. Carlos Lopez Guevara to negotiate with the leaders of San Miguelito. Juan Materno Vasquez, a black lawyer and student militant of the 1940s, was serving as secretary to the Office of the President; he later served as minister of government and justice and president of the Supreme Court. Dr. Lopez Guevara, an eminent international jurist and former minister of foreign affairs, was a close associate of the oligarchy. Torrijos would adopt this same political formula time and again when dealing with thorny problems: he would attempt to balance between "left" and "right," black and white.

The San Miguelito leadership issued several demands: (1) re-establishment of individual constitutional rights within seven days; (2) a civilian junta, with the stipulation that the junta appoint experienced and honorable individuals to work on an electoral code and hold elections no later than one year from the date of the finished electoral document; (3) that the government desist from sending international communiques affirming that there was good order in the Republic when in reality no order or respect existed for the present regime.[19]

Position papers and demonstrations notwithstanding, when the Torrijos-led government spokesmen entered into direct dialogue with leaders of San Miguelito, the main points of discussion were not restoration of individual freedom for all citizens or return to normalcy, but rather the creation of an experimental district in San Miguelito.

This meant that San Miguelito would be able to become somewhat fiscally solvent by raising local taxes and borrowing. It would no longer depend on the district of Panama for essential services. And finally, it would really have a degree of autonomy.

In agreeing to the experimental district in San Miguelito, Torrijos not only neutralized his government's most vocal opposition, but gained an opportunity to put into practice his concept of junta pueblo-gobierno rule.[20] The concept, coined by the military, meant military rule with local popular participation. This, of course, was contrary to the thinking of many leaders in San Miguelito who were thinking of a junta professional-pueblo type of government--that is, a people's government led and inspired by conscientious professionals.[21] This was an important ideological and politico-structural difference between the military leaders and the leaders of San Miguelito.

Organization of the San Miguelito District

In 1968, however, Torrijos had no administrative mechanism to implement the junta pueblo-gobierno concept. It was not until 1969 that such a mechanism was created--DIGEDECOM. "On June 3, 1969, a new Office of the Presidency was created by Cabinet Decree known as DIGEDECOM [General Directorate for Community Development], whose purpose it was to supervise and direct the Community Development programs of the national government."[22]

Once DIGEDECOM was established, preparation for self-rule under government supervision began. Former members of MUNDO were hired as DIGEDECOM employees in San Miguelito, while others were hired as community organizers by a now solvent MUNDO. The project for a special San Miguelito district was designed by members of these two agencies, and by December 1969, plans for the implementation of the district were well under way.

On December 7, 1969, Father Mahon sent a memorandum to General Torrijos in which he explained that community participation was necessary in the decisions that affected its destiny; anything to the contrary would be seen as paternalism. The memo stressed the need for a special committee to perform key functions in the implementation of the plan. Father Mahon requested that Jose Arrocha and Rafael Medina of DIGEDECOM and Eric De Leon of the Presidential Planning Office be assigned to work full-time on the San Miguelito project. All were former members of the *cursillos* and personal confidants of Father Mahon.[23] The request was promptly granted by Torrijos.

Although Torrijos gave support to the San Miguelito plan, he had reservations as to its feasibility. His skepticism was quite visible as he addressed a special meeting of San Miguelito community residents called to approve the plan and elect temporary representatives. At that meeting, held on January 25, 1970, Torrijos said,

> When various leaders of the community, together with Father Mahon, approached the Government to suggest the implementation of this plan, even though I was in complete agreement with it, I had fears that the plan might fail; San Miguelito is a community where political agitation has too often deceived the people. San Miguelito is a community that will not tolerate another deception. It is a community where demagoguery has done too much harm. The community of San Miguelito is psychologically conditioned to work for itself. This experiment in which we have so much faith, if it fails, is not your failure of Father Leon nor the failure of General Torrijos, but rather the failure of what is perhaps the last hope of doing something for this community.[24]

In spite of Torrijos's doubts as to the success of the experiment, he named Manuel Balbino Moreno, at that time controller general of the Republic, as national coordinator of DIGEDECOM, with special powers to act on San Miguelito. The appointment of Mr. Moreno to DIGEDECOM strengthened that agency's influence over the implementation of the San Miguelito plans. For instance, in negotiating whether the mayor of San Miguelito was to be elected or appointed, Mr. Moreno insisted that the mayor be appointed, at least for the first period, by the Ministry of Government and Justice. This was an important gain by the government over the community, for the mayor's role in the implementation of the plan was very crucial.[25]

Article 4 of Cabinet Decree 258 of July 30, 1969, established that "The Municipal Administration of San Miguelito will be constituted by a Community Assembly, a Municipal Council and a Mayor." Articles 5 through 9 dealt with the Community Assembly, which was composed of 68 members, one from each sector. Articles 10 through 12 dealt with the composition and functions of the Municipal Council composed of 15 councilmen and their alternates, and one municipal representative for each of the four sectors. Articles 13 through 14 dealt with the mayor and his functions. And finally Articles 21 through 28 dealt with the Administrative Tribunal.

According to Articles 13 and 14, the mayor was chief of the Municipal Administration and would be appointed by the executive body. He would have two alternates. His functions were to preside over the Municipal Council; legally represent the municipality; submit proposed agreements to the Municipal Council, particularly with respect to the budget; submit for the consideration of the Municipal Council the creation of municipal enterprises for economic and industrial development; submit for the consideration of the Community Assembly proposed agreements to assess taxes, contributions, rents, rights, and rates, according to the law, in order to cover the cost of administration and municipal services; and promote urban development in accordance with scientific planning. In short, the mayor was to be more like a business manager and less like a traditional Panamanian mayor who was usually involved in day-to-day community politics and in dispensing justice.

There was a great concentration of initiative in the office of the mayor, but this should be no surprise since, in a way, it was congruent with the concepts of _junta pueblo-gobierno_ of the Torrijos regime and _junta professional-pueblo_ of Eric De Leon. The conflict arose over whether San Miguelito would have a clientele relation along _junta pueblo-gobierno_ lines or along _junta professional-pueblo_ lines. That is, would San Miguelito's experiment be controlled by the military or its mediating structure, DIGEDECOM, or would it fall under church-sponsored groups, such as MUNDO?

MUNDO and Mahon were insistent in having a say as to who would be the first mayor and so was the government. A compromise was worked out when both sides agreed that Mahon would submit three names from which Torrijos would approve one. Mahon's first choice, Paulino Salazar, was chosen. But the precedent was set: Torrijos had appointed the mayor and hence held the right to remove him.

Salazar, an engineer and local businessman with contacts abroad, seemed a good choice in resolving the administrative and developmental problems of San Miguelito. His first challenges were to get state services to the municipality of San Miguelito in an orderly, regular, efficient manner and to set up local mechanisms to coordinate those services.

Before the enactment of Decree 258, the several hundred societies in San Miguelito received services directly from the various national ministries and agencies.[26] For example, Sr. Reluz, president of a sector called "Silos del Ife", called a meeting at which Judge Vargas, the new chief judge of the Administrative Tribunal, was present. Sr. Reluz said,

> The problem is that the streets in this community are in terrible condition. In the past, we used to contact the Ministry of Public Works and they would send us a road grader and some materials. We would put in the rest of the materials and manpower. In September 1970, we sent a letter to the Ministry in which we requested a list of materials, including cement, iron, rods, gravel, etc. Everything was approved, but we heard nothing more from them. So we wrote again January of 1971, and we received a letter dated January 29, saying that, "in accordance with the Cabinet Decree creating the District of San Miguelito, all requests for materials should be channeled through the mayor's office." This society has worked with the Municipal Government from the start. We have among us three members of the Area Council, including Sr. Orocu who is also a member of the Municipal Council. But, in October of 1970, we tried to get those materials through the municipality and we were told that funds were not yet budgeted for public works. One of my friends in the Ministry is always asking me why the Municipality is not giving us these things. I do not know what to say to him.[27]

As was later made clear by Judge Vargas, the Municipal Council had budgeting priorities, but it was precisely the ordering of those priorities that Sr. Reluz was angry about. Before Decree 258, there was no Area Council that superseded the societies; there was no Municipal Council that approved projects presented by the mayor and whose projects superseded those of the societies. And further, the presidents of the societies had previously had direct contacts in the ministries who did them favors. Many societies were discontented with the results of Decree 258.[28]

In the absence of the societies, public works coordination at the municipal level was nonexistent. And Salazar, against the desires of many councilmen, requested the establishment of nine Public Works Commissions to coordinate the work previously done by the several hundred societies. Administratively, this idea was a good one, for neither the sector representatives nor the area and municipal councilmen had the time to devote to the actual coordination of detailed public works projects. Politically, however, the commissions were in conflict with the many societies and they remained that way until the experimental scheme came to an end in August 1972, when national elections were held for a new legislative body called the National Assembly of Community Representatives.

The Gallegos Case

In a real sense, the experimental district of San Miguelito was the result of an accord between General Torrijos and Father Leo Mahon. The success of the experiment depended to a great extent on whether good church-state relations--specifically relations between Torrijos and Mahon--could be maintained. In any event, the military regime would seek to control the direction of San Miguelito politics. In ways that no one could have predicted, the Gallegos affair, which was unconnected to San Miguelito, would strain church-state relations and have a fundamental effect on the course of the experiment.[29]

Father Hector Gallegos, a Colombian priest working in Santa Fe de Veraguas, disappeared in June 1971.[30] Almost immediately, church-state relations were strained; Mahon-Torrijos cooperation came to a halt, and the San Miguelito experiment changed course.

Santa Fe de Veraguas is one of the poorest districts in Panama.[31] In the mid-1960s, many activist priests and Peace Corps volunteers began working with the peasants there. They organized marketing and consumer cooperatives as a way of breaking, or at least crippling, the economic exploitation of the peasants by the wealthier landholders and as a way of breaking the bonds of the clientele relations in the area. As in most districts, the wealthier people of Santa Fe owned the marketing and distributing facilities, and therefore reacted negatively to the attempts at encouraging the peasants to form cooperatives. The landholders often red-baited both priests and Peace Corps volunteers, but the organizing efforts continued. The conflict intensified in 1971. The main personalities of the conflict were Father Gallegos and Torrijos's landholding cousin, Alvaro Vernaza.[32]

Although there is not much background detail on the early conflict, it appears that the Torrijos regime was aware of the situation and attempted to do something about it. In early May 1971 the government met with Father Gallegos and others to discuss the possibility of setting up an experimental district along the lines of San Miguelito. The plan was called the Santa Fe plan.[33]

Torrijos was clearly seeking a solution to the class conflict in Santa Fe de Veraguas; however, in choosing San Miguelito as a model, he and his advisors did not see that political autonomy was not enough to solve the deep-seated relation of exploitation between peasants and landlords in Santa Fe. Besides, the landlords would never, if left alone, concede political power to the peasants.

Although the Santa Fe plan called for political representation for the peasantry, the traditional political leaders presented Gallegos with a slate that did not include one single peasant leader. Gallegos protested to the national government.[34] On May 22 Gallegos's bamboo hut was burned to the ground by unknown individuals, and on June 9 the newspaper La Critica (government-controlled) reported that "disguised members of the intelligence unit of the National Guard" had placed Father Gallegos under arrest and forced him to leave the mountain community with them by jeep. Gallegos has not been found and is presumed dead.[35]

As a result of Gallegos's "disappearance," church-state relations froze, and Torrijos faced his first major organized opposition since the early days after the October 11 coup.

The Catholic clergy demanded an impartial investigation of the Gallegos case. Monsignor Martin Legarra, Bishop of Veraguas, asked the Torrijos government for permission to bring a group of Mexican investigators to Panama. The Monsignor cited a precedent in the Remon assassination in 1955, when Mexican investigators were called to Panama. In spite of the precedent, Juan Materno Vasquez, minister of government and justice, denied the permit on grounds that introducing foreign investigators to Panama would put in doubt Panamanian authorities' capabilities to administer justice at a time when Panama was claiming to have those rights in the Canal Zone.[36] It was evident from his reply that the government's strategy in dealing with the issue would be to invoke the priority of national interest over all other interests.

In light of Materno Vasquez's response, the church organized all of its internal forces and orchestrated external support to pressure the regime. For example, letters of protest were sent by Colombian Catholics to the regime; letters of support came from the secretary of the Vatican, Cardinal Villot; Mons. Marcos McGrath, powerful Archbishop of Panama, visited the Vatican; and the church held an open-air mass on July 18 at Iglesia del Carmen (Church of the Bourgeoisie). MaGrath also organized a massive demonstration of 15,000 people.[37] The Torrijos regime played down the demonstration, but was quick to point out that many oligarchical and ex-political figures were among the front-line supporters of the church-organized demonstration. Torrijos argued that the oligarchy was using the church's demonstration to weaken the government's negotiating position with the United States over the canal issue.

Torrijos's position was clearly drawn for all to see. Either one backed the government in recovering the "colonial enclave" or one backed the church and played into the hands of the discredited political party leaders. McGrath realized the dilemma. He could either call for more demonstrations and risk a head-on confrontation with the Panamanian people (sovereignty over the canal is stronger than Catholicism among Panamanians), or he could join Torrijos's call for national unity and heighten his and the church's credibility among the people. McGrath's subsequent visits to the United States and other countries to advocate the recovery of the "colonial enclave" point to the fact that the church had decided to back away from a confrontation with Torrijos and to join other sectors of the Panamanian community in supporting the government's anticolonial policy.

The October Eleventh Rally

At the height of the Gallegos affair, the Torrijos regime began to prepare for the consolidation and legitimization of its government and to launch what was to become the first major foreign policy offensive against U.S. presence in the Panama Canal Zone. Two things became clear to Torrijos: (1) San Miguelito-type experiments (that is, local semi-autonomous units left to themselves to organize their community) would invariably lead to class conflicts.[38] And because Torrijos's aim was to gain support of <u>all classes</u> (<u>unidad nacional</u>) and to promote social peace, he could not afford to be challenged by any major political or social group, not even the Catholic church. (2) Torrijos also saw the need for a large counterdemonstration that would express support for his canal policy and achieve convincing popular support that the church could not ignore. He thus scheduled a mass anticolonial rally for October 11, 1971.

Salazar, the mayor of San Miguelito, upon returning from the United States where he was negotiating a municipal loan for his special district, found that he could not adhere to Torrijos's policy of using community resources to mobilize residents to attend the rally.

DIGEDECOM attempted to work around Salazar by inviting several of the fifteen San Miguelito councilmen to a dinner meeting at a luxurious hotel. At that meeting, Balbino Moreno, minister of education, coordinator of the San Miguelito plan, and coordinator of the demonstration, attempted to enlist the support of these councilmen to mobilize the community on October 11.[39] Failing to accomplish their end, DIGEDECOM officials decided to try something else.

At the urging of DIGEDECOM officials, the Electoral Tribunal of the national government ruled that the new councilmen, to be elected on September 1, 1971, would be elected indirectly by the community representatives rather than directly by their community. It was thought that this method of electing the councilmen would ensure their cooperation for the October 11th affair. In an interview Ramon Hernandez, a parish staff member said, "The government was trying to get councilmen elected that it could control, but they only got one."[40] After DIGEDECOM failed to influence the outcome of the vote for Councilmen in San Miguelito, Paulino Salazar addressed the Community Assembly. He said,

> We all have our personal reasons for wanting to go to the Plaza Cinco de Mayo on October eleventh...to show our support for General Torrijos, to whom we owe our gratitude for the creation of this District; to support the principle of Panamanian sover-

> eignty in the Canal Zone...but we will all go for San Miguelito! There are some people in the National Government who are saying that the experiment in local self-government here is dangerous, that it should be stopped. But they do not realize how strong we are...so we will show them! When we march on the Plaza Cinco de Mayo in force, and they see how many of us there are, they will know that we can no longer be controlled as in the past. They are saying that this experiment is dangerous...all right, then, let them fear San Miguelito! Que tengan miedo![41]

In spite of Paulino Salazar's rhetorical support for "October Eleventh," DIGEDECOM pressured Torrijos to replace him. They did not want to run the risk of not being able to mobilize the more than 25,000 expected San Miguelito residents.

In face of immense pressure from DIGEDECOM, Salazar resigned. He was quickly replaced by Jose Arrocha, an ex-director of the San Miguelito plan, and an employee of DIGEDECOM. Belisario Frias was appointed assistant mayor to Arrocha. Frias was a powerful figure linked to the societies in San Miguelito; he was also a staunch opponent of the San Miguelito plan insofar as that plan infringed on the powers of the societies.

Although the representatives of the Community Assembly of San Miguelito were furious over Salazar's "resignation," Arrocha stayed on as mayor and enthusiastically promoted the October Eleventh demonstrations. It was said that over $33,000 was spent on refreshments and liquor for local groups in San Miguelito who supported the demonstration.[42]

San Miguelito, which had opposed the military regime in 1968, demonstrated support for that regime--specifically its anticolonial policy--on October 11, 1971. The Reverend Leo Mahon, the Catholic church, and their lay collaborators in MUNDO were replaced as community leaders by DIGEDECOM and their supporters in the societies.

The military regime had successfully dealt with the San Miguelito challenge by participating in the experiment that had provided for local popular political participation. The regime, however, went one step further and co-opted those structures by controlling the mayoral nominating process and by using the full resources of DIGEDECOM to provide the community with all kinds of resources and manpower training. In addition, it provided jobs for some of MUNDO's best cadres.

And although the government was presented with its biggest political obstacle when it got involved in the Gallegos case, Torrijos successfully dealt with the Catholic church's challenge by rallying the support of the country around his anticolonial policy.

San Miguelito's experiment in local popular participation served the regime as a model for creating the 505 local participatory bodies--*juntas comunales*--which together formed the National Assembly of Community Representatives. Ironically, much that was germane to San Miguelito's participatory model, such as the local administrative justice system and the relative autonomy of the Community Assembly, was dismantled by the regime in order to give pre-eminence to the locally elected representative and the government-appointed *corregidor*.

Before beginning a discussion of the National Assembly of Community Representatives, which institutionalized the regime's power, let us analyze the regime's agrarian politics. This is necessary if we are to understand the role played by the peasantry, the rural proletariat, and the rural petty bourgeoisie in the legitimizing process.

NOTES

1. Panama en Cifras, 1974 (Panama, 1974), pp. 54-55; Direccion de Estadistics y Censo, Censos Nacionales de 1970, 10 de Mayo de 1970, Resultados Generales (Panama, 1970), p. 3; and survey of San Miguelito conducted by Roberto Arosemena of the University of Panama, 1974.

2. For an account of the poor housing conditions in Calidonia, Chorillo, Maranon, San Miguel, and all communities of wooden tenements that were originally rented to West Indians working in the Canal Zone, see George Westerman, Urban Housing in Panama (Panama, 1955). For a current account of these and newer slum communities, such as San Miguelito, see Samuel Gutierrez, Marginalidad y Viviendas, El Problema de los "Barriadas" en al Ciudad de Panama (Panama, 1974).

3. Eric De Leon, University of Panama industrial psychologist and San Miguelito's first community planner, identified many of the owners of these lands in "Informe Sobre Posesion de las Tierras en San Miguelito" (Panama, 1971). Among them were some of Panama's most prominent oligarchical families, such as Domingo Diaz, the Arangos, Jimenez de Stagg, Goytia, Quijano, as well as Shell Company and West Indies Ltd.

4. Ibid., p. 5. The eight fincas were Santa Elena, 1,494 hectares; Pan de Azucar, 1,833; Caceres, 1,266; San Miguel de Adentro, 600; La Pulida, 516; Juan Diaz de Pacora, 25,000; Lucha Franco, 800; and Matias Hernandez, 949.

5. Interview with Ramon Hernandez of MUNDO, Summer 1973. See also Gutierrez, Marginalidad y Viviendas, p. 39.

6. See Gutierrez, Marginalidad y Viviendas, pp. 38-39; and INCAE, "San Miguelito: Case Study No. 1" (Panama, 1972), pp. 2-4. The latter is the first of a series of working papers prepared by Instituto Centroamericano de Administracion de Empresas (INCAE) under the direction of John Ickis.

7. INCAE, "Case Study No. 1," p. 4.

8. See "San Miguelito Paper," a circular prepared by the priests of San Miguelito in January 1964.

9. San Miguelito had a reputation for being lawless and dangerous--an image that was played up by the media.

10. INCAE, "Case Study No. 1," p. 4.

11. The literature on clientelism has grown significantly. However, some of the first works are yet unsurpassed: G. Foster, "The Dyadic Contract in Tzentzuutzon: Patron-Client Relationship," American Anthropologist, no. 65 (1963), pp. 1173-92; Carl Lande, "Networks and Groups in Southeast Asia," American Political Science Review (1973); John Duncan Powell, "Peasant Society and Clientelist Politics," American Political Review 24 (1970):411-25; and E.J. Hobsbawn, "Peasants and Politics," Journal of Peasant Studies 1 (1973):3-21.

12. See MUNDO, "Comision de Estudios Interdisciplinarios para el Desarrollo de la Nacionalidad, Anexo B Programa de Desarrollo de la Comunidad del Movimiento de Unificacion Nacional, Desarrollo y Orientacion" (Panama, December 1968).

13. Interview with Ramon Hernandez, April 28, 1974.

14. Ibid.

15. See Introduction to Eric De Leon, "Informe de la Investigacion Realizada Hasta la Fecha, Sobre el Centro de Produccion de Nuevo Veranillo" (Panama, circa 1970).

16. See Paul Taylor, Evaluacion del Programa de Desarrollo Comunal Urbano de Panama (Panama, 1968). In Chapter 10 of this document, the author points to the fact that officials of the Community Development Agency complained of too much AID control of the agency; see p. 35.

17. This preoccupation was voiced in an interview with Ramon Hernandez on April 28, 1974; in Eric De Leon, "Informe de la Investigacion"; and in MUNDO's unpublished document, "Exposocion de Principios," wherein it was stated that the organization felt that sufficient progress had been made in the area of "individual education" and "family solidification" and that it was time to address the following: absence or deficiency of public service, unemployment, setting up local industry, disorganization or insignificance of local commerce and the absence of legitimate politico-administrative structures in San Miguelito. The organization therefore initiated organization of a transportation cooperative and made contacts with private and governmental agencies, such as Panamanian Construction Chamber (CAPAC) and the Institute of Training and Human Resources (IFARHU).

18. Interview with Ramon Hernandez, August 12, 1974.

19. A circular issued by MUNDO dated October 18, 1968.

20. The district was legally created by Decree 258 of July 30, 1970. By this time Torrijos had consolidated his hold on the National Guard and had begun to reach out to students, peasants, and labor. Furthermore, the tactical alliance with the Party of the People was in the making.

21. Eric De Leon was convinced that the most important ingredients for the functioning of a just and efficient government were an adequate mix of professional guidance and people's participation. The view is clearly stated in his "Perspectiva de la Democracia en Panama," prepared for MUNDO's internal use in San Miguelito (September 23, 1970).

22. INCAE, "Case Study No. 1," p. 10. The predecessor of DIGEDECOM was the AID-sponsored Oficina de Desarrollo Comunal Urbano. For a history of the development of community development agencies in Panama, see Guillermo Medina, Desarrollo de la Comunidad (Panama, 1966).

23. INCAE, "Case Study No. 1," p. 12.

24. Ibid., p. 13.

25. Interview with Eric De Leon, Summer 1971.

26. The societies were self-help organizations in San Miguelito, and their leaders were pre-empted by the new structure from their political roles as brokers between the community and the national and provincial bureaucracy.

27. INCAE, "Case Study No. 2" (Panama, 1972), p. 15.

28. There was continuous friction and suspicions between the new structure and the societies. For example, a case worker of the INCAE project reported that in a meeting held in the fall of 1971, the president of one of the societies complained about the lack of funds for projects such as street repair, electricity, trash collection, and police protection. He said, "When we used to need money for a civic project, we would hold a dance." He continued, "This year there will be no dance. . . . We haven't even bothered to request a permit. I have spoken to one of my friends who is a high-ranking officer in the National Guard and he says it is all right, but there are some people here in San Miguelito who are afraid that we will fill our pockets. We refuse to be the object of suspicion." INCAE, "Case Study No. 2," pp. 15-16.

29. See Gary MacEoin, "Church-State Rift Grows in Panama," National Catholic Reporter, January 7, 1972.

30. See Dialogo Social, nos. 34-35, Special Double Issue (May-June 1972).

31. See Panama en Cifras (Panama, 1972).

32. See Jose Alvarez Icaza M., "Indignacion Popular en Panama: La Iglesia y el Regimen Militar al Borde de la Ruptura" (June 1971), circulated by L.A.P. Service, P.O. Box 12056, Washington, D.C. 20005. For a more detailed treatment of Gallegos's sojourn in Panama and the root causes of conflicts with Alvaro Vernaza, see William Zapelock, "El Caso del Padre Hector Gallegos en Panama" (Bogota, June 23, 1971), circulated by L.A.P. Service.

33. We saw but could not obtain a copy of the plan.

34. INCAE, "Case Study No. 3" (Panama, 1972), p. 6.

35. For a detailed analysis of the socioeconomic and political interests of Torrijos and his cousin, Vernaza, in the Santa Fe district and an equally detailed analysis of Gallegos's threat to those interests, see Gem Voguel, "The Gallegos Case in Panama: Why His Abduction Is Really No Mystery." This is a twelve-page document for popular distribution that circulated in Panama in the fall of 1971.

36. El Tiempo (Bogota), July 21, 1971.

37. This information was gathered from Panama's dailies and from observation while in Panama in the fall of 1971.

38. The San Miguelito municipality was unable to prevent or even successfully contain the conflicts between squatters and landlords, especially in La Pulida. La Pulida, close to the Boyd-Roosevelt Highway, was very expensive real estate and was being reclaimed by its owner in order to build expensive ranch-type houses.

39. INCAE, "Case Study No. 3," p. 3.

40. Ibid., p. 13.

41. Ibid., p. 14.

42. Much of this information came from interviews with several Panamanian social scientists during the month of May 1974.

4

The Politics of Agricultural Reform

Writing in 1974, Alfredo Acuna, the director of the Agrarian Reform Commission (CRA), described the Torrijos regime's approach toward the Panamanian peasantry:

> Following the military coup which brought a provisional junta to the head of government, the problem of agrarian reform was taken up again. The question was what to do on this matter, facing the particularities of our country. On the one hand, there is not only a North American intervention but a permanent imperialist penetration, materialized on a 1,432 square kilometer strip of land, a perfect colonial enclave in the bowels of our territory and known as the Panama Canal Zone. On the other hand, there is a people ever more conscious of its nationalist struggles, seeking the complete sovereignty of this zone as its objective. It was not only necessary to see the agrarian reform for what it meant in reaching a new social structure in the countryside and reaching a solvent demand in the economic sphere. It was also necessary to see it as a means of incorporating that broad sector of the Panamanian population into the patriotic struggle for the liberation of our people. The incorporation of this broad marginal sector of the Panamanian population into all aspects of national life could not be postponed.[1]

Yet in so mobilizing the peasants, the Torrijos regime took care not to challenge directly the rural economic structure. Instead it sought to tap underutilized land and labor and fashion them into institutions--the peasant settlements (<u>asentamientos campesinos</u>)--for the dual purpose of fostering economic development and broadening the anti-U.S. political front.

The regime also used this innovation to strengthen its general political position. **The communist Party of the People,** with whose student wing the government had already worked out an alliance, **was given control over the National Confederation of Peasant Settlements (CONAC), founded in 1970.** In return, the Party of the People gave even more support to Torrijos.

The relationship came under strain during the economic crisis of 1973-74: the regime recognized that it could not continue to favor the poor over the oligarchy without alienating the latter at a time when the government needed its support in its challenge of Washington. Simultaneously, forces in the government came to treat the settlements solely on an economic basis, thus undermining their populist political purpose.

The Making of the Alliance

The coalition between the National Guard and CONAC did not bloom automatically. **The peasant movement, which had long-standing links to the Party of the People,** had **suffered often at the hands of the military.** **Leaders** of the movement--men like **Julio Bermudez and Dario Pitti,** who were to assume the leadership of CONAC--had been through a number of struggles against both the "internal enemy" and the "external enemy." Whether it was actions by banana workers against "Mama Yunai" (the Chiriqui Land Company), or resistance by peasants against the encroachment of the Canal Zone, the Guard had been there to impose repression. Torrijos himself was well known among peasant leaders for having killed students who led peasant guerrilla struggles in Cerro Tute in 1959.[2]

More recently, some peasant leaders who supported the Party of the People had gotten on the wrong side of the Guard by supporting Arnulfo Arias in the 1968 presidential elections and opposing the coup that quickly followed it. Consequently they, along with many other leftists, suffered intense repression in the early days of the military regime. As long as Col. Boris Martinez, an avowed anticommunist, remained prominent in the junta, rapprochement between the regime and the communists would remain highly unlikely.

But Martinez was removed in February of 1969 and Torrijos established his preeminence by early 1970. Having dispersed many opponents on the left and right, and having been abandoned by the civilian members of the junta, he was ready to enter a political alliance with the Party of the People and the social forces with which it was linked, including the peasants.

What Torrijos and the leaders of the peasant movement had in common was anti-imperialism. For people like Bermudez and Pitti, whose careers had been devoted to struggles against U.S. enclaves in Panama, the anti-imperialist cause took precedence over the fight against the owners of the latifundia. They regarded Torrijos's anti-imperialism as a way of pursuing their goal of reducing foreign influence.

They did not sacrifice their social goals for nationalist ones, however. They also saw agrarian reform as a means of radicalizing the process of change in the countryside. According to the analysis of the Party of the People,[3] the Torrijos government was quite heterogeneous, composed of progressive as well as reactionary groups. The latter included the financial, agricultural, and commercial groups linked to imperialism, while the former were white collar workers, petty bourgeois elements, peasants, and workers. To force the pace of change, particularly in the countryside, it was decided to support Torrijos in conjunction with the other progressive elements of his regime.

Torrijos, on the other hand, did not see agrarian reform in such revolutionary terms. To be sure, the peasant settlements and other economic policies were expected to raise the income of rural dwellers and to provide services to rural areas for the first time. The larger economic objective was, however, quite conventional: to increase the production of grains such as rice for domestic consumption and of cash crops like sugar for export. In combination, such increases in output would reduce the ever spiralling deficit in Panama's international balance of payments.

Politically, Torrijos obviously wanted to include the peasantry in the populist alliance, to bring them into politics for the first time. But he did not wish to do so in ways that would unnecessarily disturb the oligarchy. Thus he and his associates went to great lengths to stress that nonconfrontation and class cooperation were the hallmarks of their economic <u>and</u> political policies. Torrijos himself, in his famous speech "Nunca de Rodillas," given to banana workers on May 1, 1972, said:

> Gentlemen, the agrarian reform has done nothing improper. It has done nothing but support a revolution of growing aspirations which we would do in good

> faith, or which would be done by force by the starving peasant. We have not violated property titles, although some of these have terrible reputations and one of dubious origin.[4]

Only two weeks later, Landero Perez, director general of the Agrarian Reform Commission (CRA), repeated that the government would respect private property on the condition that its use fulfilled a social function. He then discussed two political implications of this commitment:

> The task of the agrarian reform is, therefore, to be profound and sober. We will carry out this reform within the context of the Panamanian reality, that is, without confrontations.[5]

Perez also called on all producers, peasants and landlords alike, to cooperate. He urged the former to grow cash crops and the latter to become industrialists.

> [It is incumbent upon us] to begin to promote consciousness within the peasant sector of its new needs and of its incorporation within the development process as a producer, as a dynamic subject. [It is necessary] that the private sector become interested in its best contributions to industry. But all of this is an orderly process, avoiding dangerous outcomes for countries like ours, poor and burdened by the problems of underdevelopment.[6]

This approach was stated positively by the respected Panamanian economist--and a Torrijos appointee to the National Legislative Commission--Ruben Dario Herrera. Herrera believed that there was a fundamental difference between "growth" and "development." Unlike growth, development brought about redistribution of wealth. But it required a high level of consensus and enthusiastic popular support. It was the role of the state to bring about social change without great social tensions, instability, or disequilibrium, which it could do if it had a high degree of independence relative to the economically powerful sectors but did not act in ways that alienated those interests. (By implication, Herrera rejected a revolutionary strategy that entailed a direct attack on the economic elite.)[7]

The Peasant Settlements: Mobilizing Resources

This nonconfrontational approach was reflected in the way the regime accumulated the necessary land and capital for the peasant settlements.

Land. The CRA was responsible for both acquiring land and establishing the settlements. Over the 1969 to 1973 period it acquired 260 farms consisting of 357,517 hectares. The acquisitions on a year-by-year basis are shown in Table 4-1.

TABLE 4-1: Acquisition of Land for Peasant Settlements, 1969-73.

Year	No. of Farms	No. of Hectares
1969	34	27,769
1970	40	207,413
1971	53	17,023
1972	93	79,372
1973	40	25,490
TOTAL	260	357,517

Source: Agrarian Reform Commission, Report of Activities for 1973, March 1974.

There were four ways in which the CRA secured land. Most prevalent--affecting 63 percent of the land acquired by 1972--was auction. Landowners who owed the government money for back taxes agreed to give up land as a way of clearing their indebtedness.

The second most prevalent way--24 percent of the land acquired by 1972--was expropriation in return for government bonds. In this case, the government's approach depended on whether the owner of the land was Panamanian or foreign. With respect to the foreign-owned Chiriqui Land Company (now United Brands), Torrijos responded to pressure from militant banana workers and their leaders, and exerted pressure on the company to give up lands. In the end, the company agreed to transfer several thousand acres to the CRA. Vis-a-vis Panamanian landowners, such as cattle owners in Veraguas, the CRA took a softer approach. So as not to create too much anxiety among the latifundia owners, it invoked a clause of the agrarian code that allowed government expropriation[8] when an "urgent social interest" was at stake.

The third method, accounting for 12 percent of the land acquired through 1972, was donation by landowners. The fourth was outright purchase, which brought in 1 percent of the land obtained.

Either as a result of expropriation or direct purchase, the government issued at least $5.5 million in bonds which earned interest ranging from 1 to 6 percent and were redeemable anywhere from twenty to forty years. In all cases, the land acquired was not the best land of the latifundia; rather it was the marginal land occupied by squatters (precaristas). The total land acquired represented little more than 4 percent of the national territory and 4.41 percent of the useful agricultural lands.[9] Moreover, about 80 percent of the land acquired was in Panama province, whereas the country's most productive land was in the interior provinces of Chiriqui, Cocle, and Veraguas.

Capital. Financing, from both international and domestic sources, was available at reasonable cost to all but the poorest class of farmer--the very group that Torrijos sought to benefit through the peasant settlements. As a result, the regime sought to fill the gap by creating its own mechanism for capital accumulation--the Agricultural Development Bank (BDA). Ironically, the BDA received most of its funding from the U.S. Agency for International Development (AID) and international development institutions at the very time that Torrijos was attempting to renegotiate Panama's relationship with the United States in particular and the international community in general.

Prior to 1973 the main sources of agricultural credit were private banks, usually foreign-owned; private merchants; the National Bank of Panama; and the Institute of Economic Promotion (IFE).

The private banks began to build a clientele in Panama in the 1950s by servicing the needs of cattle owners and over time branched out to support all large-scale farmers, agribusiness, sugar manufacturers, and banana producers. About 60 percent of their portfolios were guaranteed with land mortgages.[10] The National Bank made loans to medium and large farmers, with a preference for cattle ranchers. The IFE, which got its funds from the Inter-American Development Bank (BID) and AID, was the only source of credit for small farmers, who had to offer crops, livestock, or equipment as collateral.

The main sources from which peasants could borrow were traditional, noninstitutional lenders, such as provincial money lenders, landlords, and shopkeepers.

Their financial activities were one way in which they preserved important political positions in rural society, and had the effect of perpetuating the poverty and powerlessness of their clients.[11]

It was with these traditional lenders that the Agricultural Development Bank was created to compete. As active as the BDA was, its purposes were not totally consistent with the international agencies--AID and the World Bank--that provided its resources. The BDA and the regime that created it wished to get capital in the hands of peasant settlers and so increase agricultural output, diminish poverty, and strengthen the political bonds between Torrijos and the poor peasant. The external agencies were concerned about economic performance of the recipient country, and sought to influence the direction, pace, and orientation of its government policies.[12] AID in particular seeks to maximize its "leverage" over recipient countries.[13]

Yet these agencies never attained anything like institutional control over the policies of the Torrijos government. Despite substantial increases in the amount of support extended, the regime was able to avoid becoming the captive of outside organizations, just as it was able to avoid being manipulated by domestic classes. The regime achieved this primarily by centralizing economic decision making and control over nonprivate capital flows in the Ministry of Planning and Economic Development. It thus maximized its own leverage over the international agencies and the process of agricultural reform.

Establishing the Peasant Settlements

The initial idea for peasant settlements was developed by the Interamerican Institute of Agricultural Sciences (IICA). The IICA conceived of the settlement (*asentamiento*) as a socioeconomic enterprise in which land was held on an individual basis but farming and other work was done on a collective basis.[14] Each settlement would consist of around fifty families.

In order to enhance the viability of the settlements as centers of new communities and to facilitate the delivery of government services, the IICA model suggested that settlements be grouped in clusters of four.[15] Administratively, each settlement would have a general assembly of all the settlers (*asentados*), and an administrative council consisting of an administrative committee, an education committee, and a security committee. The task of the latter, which reported directly to the general assembly, was to protect the settlement from encroachment by latifundia owners.[16]

The Torrijos regime made several adjustments in adapting the settlement model to Panama. In the first place, as suggested above, the settlements were regarded as vehicles for mobilizing in a controlled way poor peasant support of the regime in its anti-imperialist goals. Indeed, Torrijos the leader became the focus of peasant support. Second, the settlements were portrayed as transitory structures: after a three-to-five year period, land would be parcelled out to the peasants, who would establish cooperatives.[17] This modification was opposed by the Party of the People and CONAC, because they contended that it would weaken the peasant movement and dilute CONAC's political leadership. But it probably reflected a certain indecisiveness within the regime over how far to take the experiment, and represented a compromise between contending forces. Third, at least initially the settlements had no legal personality and could not enter into contracts with public and private entities. They were dependent on the CRA, which was their patron and guardian. As a result of CONAC pressure, however, the settlements were given legal personality in April 1972.[18]

The organization of settlements took place in three stages. The first stage, in which the leadership of CONAC was very important, lasted from a few weeks to about three months. During this period the CRA would collect personal data concerning potential beneficiaries and carry out extensive motivation and leadership conferences. Of central importance at this stage was the selection of the settlement site (the land being provided by the government). Sites invariably were in areas of great social or economic tension, such as Baru in Chiriqui, Sona in Veraguas, and Chepo-Pacora in Panama--a clear indication that political factors were as important as economic ones.

In the second stage, the settlers organized themselves into a constituent assembly and subscribed to an act of constitution. They elected a settlement committee that would represent the unit before the CRA (in 1972 the president of the settlement was given preeminence over the committee, a departure from the IICA model). Next the settlers adopted a set of internal rules that spelled out the rights and duties of each. Finally a contract, which would be the basis of a plan of production, was to be entered into with the CRA. The government was to provide credit and technical advice.[19]

In the third stage the land was to be divided among qualified settlers, property titles given to individual beneficiaries, and a cooperative set up.

CONAC as a Broker Institution

Mediating the political relationship between Torrijos and the government on the one hand, and the settlements on the other, was the National Confederation of Peasant Settlements (CONAC). Controlled by the Party of the People, CONAC set for itself two goals: first, to mobilize mass support for Torrijos; and second, to use its influence with the government to radicalize the agrarian reform process. These two goals were not necessarily mutually exclusive, but neither were they totally compatible.

In fact, the leadership of CONAC was inclined to place higher priority on supporting Torrijos in his anti-U.S. endeavors than they were in revolutionizing the countryside. Julio Bermudez, CONAC's executive secretary, and Dario Pitti, leader of the important Chiriqui settlement, had consistently guided the peasant movement on an anti-imperialist course in struggles against the foreign-owned fruit companies and against the Canal Zone itself. They held that the actual reformist and populist policies of Torrijos were tantamount to an anti-oligarchical and anti-imperialist process, thus defining away the problem. It followed that the revolutionary process should be defended at all costs, and that changes in the land tenure system were to be delayed. As an ideological corollary, Bermudez rejected the idea that the settlements were socialist in nature. Given Panama's stage of development, they could only be considered a kind of progressive capitalism.[20]

CONAC had an intermediate political goal, which was to expand the number of settlements and settlers that it represented, and so enhance its clout with Torrijos. Its hope was ultimately to represent over 80,000 families. Yet when the organization convened for its second congress in 1972, its membership consisted of only 200 settlements composed of 5,000 families. To make matters worse, government acquisition of land seemed to have peaked and was declining rapidly. Without more land for settlements, CONAC could not grow.

Consequently, forces favoring a more radical approach made themselves heard at the congress. The Subcommittee on Livestock Production passed a resolution calling for a more revolutionary program of land acquisition and demanding that the CRA enforce the "efficient utilization" clause of the 1962 agrarian code, on the grounds that the large livestock latifundia were an impediment to cattle production goals. A resolution of the Agro-Industry Subcommittee went even further: it called the code "obsolete and inadequate" to meet the needs of the peasantry and an impediment to social justice. It asserted that it was meaningless to talk of social justice for all Panamanians and the "social function" of land as long as the latifundia had an average of two acres for each head of cattle and, at the same time, thousands of families lived in misery without minimum land requirements.[21]

Those delegates at the second congress who felt that agrarian reform had not gone far enough united under the banner of "popular unity," a coalition of "progressive" forces. This faction was led by Romulo Betancourt of the FEP, and representatives from the National Workers Confederation (CNT) and the Panamanian College of Agricultural Engineers. But others at the congress, led by Father Villalobos from the church, Col. Antonio Noriega of the National Guard, the CRA director Robledo Landero, waved the banner of "national unity": the incorporation of all sectors and classes of national life, including the traditional oligarchy and its followers. The implication was that social change would be gradual at best.

Father Villalobos characterized the peasantry as "Samson awakening." He prayed that the peasantry, with its new-found strength, would build rather than destroy as Samson did. He exhorted the peasantry not to reverse the wheels of fate and exploit other social classes. His underlying message, veiled in flattery, was that the peasantry should not challenge the status quo by radicalizing the movement in order to end latifundia domination.[22]

Similarly, Noriega poetically praised the peasants for their role in the revolution but warned them against pushing too hard too soon:

> Thousands of raised machetes to defend the Revolution. . .this is the march of a people towards destiny. This is the trajectory of a people in search of their liberation, which nothing and no-one can halt. <u>We cannot, however, accelerate any process because everything marches as human beings march. They are born, they reproduce, they die. Thus are the revolutions of the people. Let us be calm. Let us not accelerate these processes</u>.[23]

Landero took another tack. He asserted that the national unity strategy would be the most effective basis for negotiating with the United States. "The general policy of the State," he said, "is primarily geared towards a search for national unity, . . . a unity which will permit us to feel as a free nation."[24] The peasantry had their role in foreign policy:

> Presently all of you are recipients of the developmental plans of the government, and that is why we have initiated programs that could be characterized as the spinal cord of the Panamanian revolution. And in search of this national sentiment which will serve as our guide in negotiations with the United States, all of you, as sectors of public opinion, will play an important role.[25]

In the end, the congress generally reaffirmed its support for Torrijos's leadership and his sacrifices for the Panamanian peasantry. It made a general appeal for a new agrarian law to be the framework for more dynamic agrarian reform. But the only specific criticism was a call on the General to remove uncooperative officials in the CRA.[26] For his part, Torrijos chose to side with neither advocates of "national unity" nor partisans of "popular unity." He assumed his favorite posture of "neither with the left, nor with the right, but with Panama," and so maintained a margin of flexibility to deal with the mix of groups and classes.[27]

The Alliance Under Stress

The relationship of the settlements with the Torrijos regime thus had all the features of political clientelism. Torrijos, the charismatic leader, was the patron who set the boundaries of the relationship. At the bottom were the clients, the settlements. Through the semiautonomous CRA, Torrijos provided them with land, credit, and a political identity in return for their political support. CONAC served the role of intermediary, gaining national political power for itself in the process as long as it did not push agrarian reform beyond the limits that suited Torrijos.

This clientelist structure could survive as long as it was not subject to too much pressure. But the economic recession of 1973 and 1974, coming as it did at the time that Torrijos was mounting a serious challenge to the United States, forced the regime to make concessions to the oligarchy in order to preserve national unity. At the same time, national bureaucracies became more influential in rural policy, and they assessed the peasant settlements more on the basis of their economic viability than on their political impact.

Torrijos's appointment of Ornel Urriola, a member of the Party of the People, as governor of Chiriqui province was a portent of the coming political crisis. Chiriqui was a province of great landed wealth and naked poverty, the place where the oligarchy and the Chiriqui Land Company (United Brands) had long wielded enormous power. Chiriqui was also the province where economically successful and politically organized settlements had emerged under the leadership of Dario Pitti. Thus threatened, the provincial oligarchs regarded Urriola as a new challenge and sought his removal. They claimed that he was using student radicals from the communist-affiliated FEP to implement "communist" reforms by distributing propaganda and intimidating educational personnel. They organized a series of demonstrations in July and August--the "Chiricanazo"--and Torrijos gave way. Urriola was replaced.

But the principal issue of conflict was which group in the agricultural sector was going to get priority recession assistance. The middle- and large-scale farmers felt that they had been short-changed by the agricultural reform. They would have no doubt agreed with the following retrospective analysis of the regime's economic policies by the Committee for Inter-American Alliance (CIAP):

> A government attack on . . . rural problems began in 1969. Unfortunately, however, the lack of a comprehensive policy meant that the progress made was at the cost of creating new difficulties or aggravating existing problems. The government sought to organize poor farmers in groups (settlements, production councils, cooperatives) which received priority treatment in respect to technical, financial and physical resources of the public sector for their socio-economic development. This resulted initially in uncertainty and some neglect in the servicing of medium and large-scale commercial farmers, who account for most of the marketed agricultural output.[28]

Through 1973 and 1974 the regime took a number of steps to deal with the economic problems of those in the countryside who believed they had been disadvantaged by past policy. The first step was a reorganization of the national ministries. A Ministry of Planning and Economic Policy was set up with Nicolas Ardito Barletta at its head to rationalize decision making and the allocation of resources. The Ministry of Agriculture and Livestock was transformed into the Ministry of Agricultural Development (MIDA). The Agrarian Reform Commission (CRA), which had been instrumental in setting up the peasant settlements, became the National Department for Agricultural Reform (DINRA) and lost most of its autonomy to MIDA. And it was at this time that all agricultural credits were concentrated in the Agricultural Development Bank. As far as agriculture was concerned, these changes were designed to give the regime greater control of policy with respect to marketing, pricing, credit, industrial processing of agricultural products, agricultural reform, and the development of different types of cooperatives.

Thus reorganized, the regime then responded to a CIAP recommendation that MIDA draw up a five-year plan with specific targets for finance, credit, and technical resources to be provided, and allocate those on the basis of soil conditions, technical capacity, and financial condition of the farmer. To increase production, MIDA promoted an increased use of modern inputs, particularly machines and fertilizer. Imports of equipment and machines increased by over 40 percent in 1974. The government also sought to build the rural infrastructure--roads, electric power, and water resources.

This shift in policy was reflected in the government's 1974 budget for agriculture. The current-expense budget, which mainly benefited small farmers and the peasant settlements, was unchanged from the 1973 amount of $9.5 million. The investment budget, which went for infrastructure and machinery, reached a new high of $21.2 million, $11.7 million of which was borrowed from foreign banks.[29]

These production-oriented policies tended to work against the peasant settlements. As a result of centralization, MIDA set their production plans and made it difficult to diversify. A settlement leader in Cocle said in an interview that he "almost had a fight with Gerardo Gonzalez, the head of MIDA, because of the tight control which the ministry exercised over the settlement."[30] With the exception of the unit in Chiriqui, the settlements were least likely to have the kind of land, technical level, and financial condition to merit government resources once they were provided on a purely economic calculus. To the extent that the settlements began using machines and fertilizers, the oil crisis caused the costs of production to rise quickly. The price of a ton of fertilizer jumped from $120 in 1973 to over $300 in 1974; the cost of rice production rose by more than 50 percent. As a result, many settlers went deeply into debt, which the Agricultural Development Bank was either unwilling or unable to remedy. The combination of these factors caused many to abandon the settlements in search of alternatives, such as employment on latifundias or with state-owned or transnational agribusiness.[31]

CONAC was impotent in the face of this crisis. One informant said that CONAC was ineffective because it had little information as to what was going on, and that furthermore CONAC was financially beholden to MIDA. Politically, the leadership was unwilling to hold Torrijos to account. Dario Pitti supported MIDA policies as the only way to solve the crisis.[32] Of Julio Bermudez, a Cocle informant said, "At first he and others would come and talk to us about organizing, but now they remain in the cities talking to the ministers."[33] A more profound problem afflicting CONAC was that Torrijos --the patron--**maintained direct contact with his clients at the grass roots (the settlers) and enjoyed their confidence.** Even in the midst of the economic crisis the settlers generally expressed faith in Torrijos's good will and his capacity to solve their problems. His ability to bypass the CONAC leadership and offer solutions **to peasant problems weakened CONAC as a political broker and diminished its bargaining power vis-a-vis Torrijos.**

The economic crisis continued to deepen in 1974. The annual growth rate dropped to less than 4 percent, half of the 1960s rate. The inflation rate was more than 25 percent a year, with food prices rising so fast that grocers' price lists were written on blackboards rather than being printed. Panama's debt per capita continued upward, becoming the highest in Latin America. As the international price of sugar fell, the huge government investments in sugar installations were at risk.

The oligarchy saw its opportunity to reverse some of the regime's policies and create trouble for Torrijos's coalition in the process. CONEP decried the fact that:

> There are other important economic policies such as labor policies, agrarian reform, price controls, and the assignment of relative and different roles to different types of economic organization (State enterprises, cooperatives, and private enterprise) in the national structure which are as important as, if not more important than, those pertaining, within the scope of the new legislation, strictly to private investment.[34]

CONEP had welcomed the new emphasis on infrastructure and basic services. But it wanted a redefinition of the state's role in the economy. It sought a modification of the regime's support for the settlements and its enforcement of the labor code of 1972 (which called for compulsory unionization, job security, etc.). CONEP was not happy about the state's acquisition of the Cerro Colorado Copper Mine, its increased participation in agribusiness (particularly sugar), and its ownership of the hydroelectric plant.

Conscious of his need for the support of all Panamanians on the canal issue, Torrijos answered these criticisms in his famous "Boquete Declaration" in November 1974. He offered a compromise with the private sector, focusing particularly on the food and livestock industry and the stagnant construction industry. To stimulate production by large-scale producers, the government granted substantial increases in the prices those farmers received for their marketed goods. Torrijos also offered fiscal incentives to promote reinvestment, subsidies and low interest rates for those investing in construction and agriculture, loan guarantees and a ten-year freeze in real estate taxes on new construction, and reductions in the tariffs on certain nontraditional exports.[35]

At the same time, MIDA was undertaking a fundamental reassessment of the peasant settlements. An internal MIDA report asserted that although 1974 had seen an increase in the output of rice (attributed to the production-oriented policies described above), the settlements had had only limited success in raising the settlers' standard of living. In MIDA's eyes, the settlements had the following problems:

--a great number had poor land to work with at a time that production costs were increasing, and many were still without land.

--they had gotten significant supplies of credit from the BDA only since 1972.

--few, if any, had irrigation or drainage, and roads for marketing were severely lacking.

--they were exploited by speculators (MIDA bought as little as a quarter of their output).[36]

MIDA did not recommend a more radical program of land acquisition and distribution. Rather it proposed to incorporate the economically viable settlements into an arrangement that bordered on state capitalism. The settlements were to be consolidated into multipurpose agricultural firms (empresas multiples agrarias), and their output was to be bought up by a new system of state-sponsored agribusinesses run by the municipal governments. In the process, their economic independence would be further compromised; their populist political role would be greatly emasculated.

NOTES

1. Alfredo V. Acuna H., *Aspectos de la Reforma Agraria Panamena* (Panama, 1974), p. 13. Emphasis added.

2. Interviews with leaders of peasant settlements (*asentamientos*) in Baru district of Chiriqui province, particularly with Dario Pitti and Almengor and D. Sanchez, March 1974.

3. In a 1970 document, the party established that the oligarchy was the principal instrument of imperialism, the fundamental enemy of the people. Hence, the primary responsibility of the Panamanian revolution was the liquidation of the oligarchy. See Ruben Dario Souza, et al., *Panama 1903-1970* (Santiago, 1970). In a 1973 document, the party recognized that the 1968 military coup created objective conditions that favored the development of both mass action and mass organizations. See Ruben Dario Souza, "Formacion de la Lucha Anti-Imperialista en Panama y el Papel de los Comunistas" (unpublished, 1973). It is this assessment of the strategic enemy and the political conjuncture that led the party to ally itself with the Torrijos regime. See also Carlos Nunez, "Panama: El Reformismo de los Militares," *Pensamiento Critico*, no. 41 (June 1970), pp. 208-19.

4. Omar Torrijos, *La Batalla de Panama* (Buenos Aires, 1973), p. 111.

5. "IV Reunion Interamericana de Ejecutivos de Reforma Agraria" (Proceedings of a conference held by Interamerican Executives for Agrarian Reform, Panama, May 14-20, 1972), p. 53.

6. Ibid., p. 54.

7. See Ruben Dario Herrera P., *La Necesidad de Cambios Sociales en el Desarrollo Economico de Panama*, no. 2 (Panama, 1974).

8. Acuna, *Aspectos de la Reforma*, p. 7.

9. Ibid., p. 9.

10. See William C. Merrill et al., *Panama's Economic Development: The Role of Agriculture* (Iowa, 1975), p. 164; and Robert Looney, *The Economic Development of Panama* (New York, 1976), p. 100.

11. See Marco Gandasegui, "Cambio Social en el Agro," in Documento del II Congreso de Sociologia (Panama, 1976), p. 39.

12. See Union of Radical Political Economy, vol. 9, no. 4, p. 49.

13. See Theresa Hayter, Aid as Imperialism (England, 1971), p. 87.

14. See Federico Herrero, Guia para la Elaboracion de un Programa de Reforma Agraria 1 and 2 (Guatemala, 1973); and also various country studies conducted by IICA in Chile, Venezuela, Panama, and Colombia, such as "Las Empresas Comunitarias Campesinas" (circa 1973).

15. Interview with Federico Herrero at IICA offices, April 1974.

16. Herrero, Guia para la Elaboracion, p. 74.

17. Interview with a senior economist of the Agrarian Reform Commission, May 1974.

18. Ibid.

19. In 1972, at the Second Congress of the Asentamientos Campesinos, the representatives threatened to reject the CRA's production plans. Representatives from Baru, Chiriqui did not join the action. The representatives had complained of having no participation in drawing up production plans. See Mario Melo Suarez, Las Empresas Comunitarias Campesinas en Panama (Bogota, 1972), p. 42.

20. Interview with Julio Bermudez, 1974.

21. See proceedings of the Second Congress of CONAC, held February 9-11, 1972, in Memoria de la CONAC (Panama, 1973). The 1962 Agrarian Reform Law has many loopholes that are favorable to large landholders, especially Articles 12 and 41; see Looney, The Economic Development of Panama, p. 101.

22. Memoria de la CONAC, p. 1.

23. Quoted in El Panama America, August 15, 1971.

24. Memoria de la CONAC, p. 4.

25. Ibid., p. 2. Emphasis added.

26. Memoria de la CONAC, resolutions 3 and 4 of the Subcommittee on Miscellaneous.

27. Another way of playing "right" against "left" was to allude to patriotism. In his famous 1971 speech before two hundred thousand persons, Torrijos said, "We are looking for our own solution, the right medicine for our people; the right aspirin for our own headache. A Panamanian does not go out with an umbrella when it is raining in Moscow. This is a lie. A Panamanian does not put on an overcoat when it is snowing in Washington. This is a lie." Torrijos, La Batalla de Panama, p. 88.

28. CIAP, Panama Report (Panama, 1974), p. 82.

29. See Memoria del MIDA 1974, annual report presented to ANRC (Panama, 1974), pp. 8-9.

30. Interview with the representative from Rio Hato Sur, August 1974.

31. Even in Baru where the settlements had been more successful, the asentados claimed that they did not have work for more than six months of the year, and that they had to seek employment elsewhere. In Veraguas and Cocle many of the asentados interviewed had already sought employment at state-owned sugar mills, and many had expressed interest in seeking employment at the government-built fishmeal and processing plants at Vacamonte. The degree of land concentration and squatter problems in the banana zone in Panama is well documented by Ana Pitti and Omar Jaen Suarez in "La Propiedad de la Tierra en Panama," Dialogo Social, no. 21 (October 1970), pp. 18-19.

32. Interview with Dario Pitti, January 1975.

33. Interview with the president of the Rio Hato Sur settlement, August 1974. For an analysis of how peasant leaders become bureaucrats, see Gerrit Huizer, El Potencial Revolucionario del Campesino en America Latina (Mexico, 1973), p. 284.

34. INDESA, Boletin Informativo, no. 5 (September 1974).

35. See "Declaracion de Boquete," Tareas, no. 41 (January-March, 1978), anexo 1; and Matutino, November 30, 1974, p. 16b.

36. MIDA, "Empresas Multiples Agrarias" (Panama, 1974).

5

Institutionalization of the Revolution: A New National Constitutional Structure

San Miguelito and the peasant settlements represented significant attempts to draw the poorest of the poor in both city and countryside into the political process. But that was no substitute for a constitutional structure that would both realize Torrijos's vision of the popular alliance's political role and enhance the regime's legitimacy. Only days after the October Revolution, the military had disbanded the National Assembly and political parties that were the institutional expression of the oligarchy's customary power. Torrijos subsequently toyed with the idea of a one-party system as employed in other Latin American nations. But in the early seventies he chose a representative structure, in which elected representatives of the people at each level of administration were to balance the power of appointed executives. The new system was embodied in a constitution that was drafted and ratified in 1972.

Having proposed to open new channels of participation, the regime had to ensure that the resulting demands on the system would not jeopardize its policies, undermine its power, or deprive it of flexibility. At the central level, the National Assembly of Community Representatives (NACR) sought to expand its power and influence from the time it gathered to ratify the new constitution. Yet it was generally more successful in generating support for Torrijos than articulating demands on him and his lieutenants. Similarly, representatives at the local level were usually unable to overcome the traditional monopoly of power enjoyed by the appointed _corregidor_.

This chapter describes the representatives' struggle for meaningful political participation at the national level, and the following chapter describes what occurred at the local level.

Drafting the Constitution: Ideology and Structure

Torrijos charged a Commission on Constitutional Reforms with writing a charter to replace the constitution of 1946. The commission was predominantly professional and middle class. Out of a membership of twenty-seven, four members were professors, three had doctoral degrees, one was a medical doctor, one was a retired colonel, five were engineers, five were businessmen, five were attorneys, and two were labor lawyers. The leadership role was taken by four attorneys: Aristides Royo, Adolfo Ahumada, Ricardo Alonso Rodriguez, and Marcelino Jaen. The first three were former members of the students' federation, and Jaen was a brother-in-law of Torrijos.[1]

The Commission on Constitutional Reforms worked within an ideological framework defined by the military and the hybrid executive-legislative National Legislative Commission (NLC). In October 1973 Rodriguez publicly and retrospectively described the four concepts that had guided the commission's work: revolution, social justice, democracy, and sovereignty.[2]

"Revolution" meant a national transformation so that all sectors of the Republic could participate in its well-being and its national riches. That transformation had to be institutionalized--given a juridical basis--to promote development and combat the structures of injustice in an orderly and responsible manner.

"Social justice" within the revolution meant the recognition and extension of rights for children, youth, women, workers, people of Indian origin, and peasants. Operationally, this required guarantees of the right of workers to organize, of job security, and of protection against arbitrary dismissals; respect for indigenous reservation lands; greater priority placed on education and health for all; and dedication of greater resources for agricultural development, including the peasant settlements.

"Democracy" was to be achieved without Western-style institutions. Political parties and parliaments were judged to be alien and unrepresentative of the interests of the masses, and furthermore, to contribute to disorder. Panama required structures of permanent political consultation that would facilitate community participation in all important decisions, as well as foster a climate of order and harmony between social classes, races, and political interests.[3]

"Sovereignty" was defined simply as the political, social, cultural, and economic integration of the Canal Zone within the nation-state--the central political objective of at least three generations of Panamanians.

Above all, the revolution was conceived of as a pragmatic undertaking that rejected ideologies such as capitalism, socialism, and communism.[4] It should be a national and flexible effort, led by General Torrijos and the National Guard, and embracing a broad alliance of workers, students, peasants, and other progressive forces. Anyone who deviated from the ends of the revolution or objected to the means employed were regarded as collaborators with the oligarchy or members of the ultra-left.[5]

By mid-1972, the Commission on Constitutional Reforms had completed a draft document. The structure, which was termed the "people-government administration" (<u>junta pueblo-gobierno</u>) envisaged the following elements:

--at the national level, executive leadership would be vested in General Torrijos and legislative power shared by the elected National Assembly of Community Representatives and the National Legislative Council (CNL). (The CNL should not be confused with the National Legislative Commission [NLC], a pre-existing hybrid, executive-legislative body that served as the ideological and political vanguard of the populist corporatist process.)

--at subnational levels (the province, the district or municipality, and the <u>corregimiento</u>), elected representatives and specified appointed executive officials would form a governing council.[6]

Administratively, Panama was composed of 505 <u>corregimientos</u> (a unit that survived from Spanish colonial times), which were aggregated into sixty-four districts, which themselves formed nine provinces plus the autonomous Cuna Indian area of San Blas. A representative (<u>representante</u>) was to be elected in each <u>corregimiento</u> and preside over the community board of that unit. The representative and the local <u>corregidor</u> would constitute the people-government administration. The representatives of each district were to form a municipal body (<u>municipio</u>), headed by the government-appointed mayor. The representatives of each province were to be members of a provincial coordinating council along with the governor and the heads of all government agencies.

As to the national level, the draft constitution clearly concentrated power in the hands of General Torrijos. For the transition period of 1972 to 1978, he was to have the power to:

--coordinate public administration;

--appoint and remove ministers of state, NLC members, the national-level controller and assistant controllers, general-directors of autonomous and semiautonomous agencies, and magistrates of the electoral tribunal;

--designate heads and officers of the public security force according to the constitution and the military law;

--appoint, with the approval of the executive council, magistrates of the Supreme Court;

--appoint the attorney general;

--negotiate contracts and loans;

--and direct the foreign policy of the nation.

Torrijos would also have the right of voice and vote in meetings of the executive council and the CNL, and the right of voice in the NACR, provincial coordinating councils, and the community boards.[7]

Article 141 of the draft constitution specified that the 505 members of NACR, one from each of the *corregimientos*, were to meet in October each year. The assembly was to exercise the following powers: election of the president and vice president of the country; approval or rejection of international treaties, which the executive had the authority to negotiate; declare war or peace; approve or reject the redrawing of political subdivisions, as proposed by the CNL; proclaim amnesty for political prisoners; and draw up its own internal rules. As set forth in Articles 146 and 148, all the other legislative functions were reserved to the CNL, which was composed of the president and vice president of the Republic, the president of the NACR, the ministers of state, and all the members of the NLC. Since Torrijos had the power of appointment and removal of all of the members of the CNL, except for the president and vice president of the Republic and the NACR president, the legislative power was in effect to be in the hands of the executive.[8]

Preparations for the Constituent Assembly

The first responsibility of the NACR was to act as a constitutent assembly, by ruling on the draft prepared by the Commission on Constitutional Reforms. Elections were scheduled for August 1972.

In preparing for the elections, the government turned to DIGEDECOM, which since 1969 had provided local communities with funding for a variety of community programs, and so establishing a beachhead for the regime at the lowest social level (see Chapter 4). With funding from AID, the agency devoted most of its resources during the period of late 1971 and early 1972 to preparing and organizing communities for the 1972 elections. DIGEDECOM members in effect played the role that party cadres play in party systems.

Based on its experience and contact with rural communities, DIGEDECOM began offering a number of leadership seminars to rural and urban community groups. It also conducted a number of structured community-level socioeconomic surveys that were used to measure how the community judged its own leadership. Through both the seminars and the surveys, DIGEDECOM identified and gave support to many candidates who were later elected as representatives.[9]

In some exceptional cases, DIGEDECOM had to take extraordinary steps to reduce resistance to the new system. One of these was the Renacimiento area of Chiriqui province. This region had favored Arnulfo Arias in the 1968 election and was a base for the brief armed resistance to the coup. DIGEDECOM and the Agricultural Development Bank made possible the building of a fourteen-kilometer road from Renacimiento to Rio Sereno. Farmers could get their cattle to market and so were more inclined to support the regime.

The representatives elected were a cross section of the peasantry, middle-level farmers, and urban working class. (As later became apparent, the principal cleavage among the representatives was between those from rural and urban areas.) Over 70 percent of the national assembly--350 representatives--were either nationalist or pro-Torrijos; sixty delegates were members of the Party of the People; fifty were former members of the traditional political parties; forty-four were independents; and one was a Christian Democrat.[10] For the first time in a Panamanian legislature, there were two representatives from the Canal Zone, reflecting the more confrontational approach of the Torrijos regime toward the United States.

In advance of the convening of the assembly, the regime sought to ensure that there would be no surprises. Torrijos and other officials met with the various provincial delegations in late August to install them and give them their credentials.[11] Members of the Commission on Constitutional Reforms led seminars at the Institute of Training and Human Resources (IFARHU) in Tocumen for the representatives.

Then in early September the political opposition, mainly members of the displaced political oligarchy, engaged in a last-minute attempt to discredit the assembly and undermine Torrijos's effort to broaden the legitimacy of his regime. Rumors were circulated that the assembly's mandate was not to replace the 1946 constitution but merely to modify it. Adolfo Ahumada, one of the leading figures on the Commission on Constitutional Reforms, quickly and publicly refuted the allegation and asserted that both legally and politically, the convocation was fully qualified to serve as a constituent assembly. For the most part, the representatives were reassured about the importance of their role.[12]

The Constitutional Debate

Yet the representatives were far from docile during the assembly debate over the constitution. Although they were willing to accept a subordinate status within the populist alliance, they still tried to push the military and the civilian professionals in the government to adopt a more progressive position on major economic, social, and political questions. More importantly, they attempted to broaden the channels of participation and so gain greater decision-making power for the NACR and for its counterparts at the provincial and district levels.

Expanding the NACR's Legislative Powers. The assembly began by passing a resolution to reject categorically the $1.9 million canal annuity from the United States. Without much objection, it suspended its internal rules and approved the extraordinary powers for the "chief" (*jefe*), General Torrijos. The representatives then listened as the general tried during his acceptance speech to convince them that he would share his powers with them and make no important decision without consulting with them.[13]

It was unclear to the representatives, however, how that consultation would take place and therefore what its impact would be. Who would be consulted? When? On what issues? By what mechanism?

What was clear from the draft constitution was that, in spite of Torrijos's statement to them that "you are the ones who are going to legislate,"[14] was that most of the legislative power was vested in the CNL, which the general controlled by virtue of his appointment powers. Responding to questions, Torrijos asserted that the representatives' participation would "be by way of permanent consultation taking place at the provincial level within the provincial coordinating council."[15] The problem was that Torrijos could choose when and if to consult these bodies; by consulting each of the nine councils separately, he could make it difficult for them to exert any collective pressure vis-a-vis the chief executive. Some representatives took refuge in Article 145 of the draft constitution, which stated that laws made by the NACR should be proposed by special commissions of the NACR or by the CNL. But the dominant view was that Article 141, which stated specifically the few powers the NACR was allocated, took precedence.

There ensued a series of motions designed to expand the assembly's role. Several sought to place NACR members on the NLC, automatically making those so placed on the CNL, which was correctly perceived as the real locus of legislative power. The first was introduced by Ernesto Cordoba, whose constituency was Las Cumbres in Panama. He proposed that beginning in 1978 the NACR select from its own membership two or three representatives per province to sit on the NLC. If adopted, that proposal would have changed dramatically the composition of the professional-dominated NLC and might have given those popularly elected a majority within the CNL. Cordoba's motion was defeated, as were similar ones by Eberto Anguizola, who represented cattle owners, and by labor leader Dario Pitti. Some opponents of the initiatives argued that they would detract from Torrijos's power to carry out the revolution, and others accused the proponents of aspiring to the "privileged caste."[16] In general, representatives from rural areas were disinclined to limit Torrijos's power.

Next came a proposal by Gerardo Mojica from San Miguelito to create an executive committee of the NACR to sit in Panama City and serve as a communications link between the predominantly rural representatives and the hard-to-find bureaucrats in the urban-based ministries and public agencies. Torrijos felt moved to respond by admonishing Mojica and his colleagues to have more confidence in him as the element unifying all classes and the mediator of all group or class conflicts within the populist alliance. The general asserted that an executive committee of the NACR would not solve the problem of the inaccessible bureaucrat. He said:

> Whether you are taken care of or not does not depend on a formal link but on attitude. So when you want to guarantee through such a link that you will be heard, I get the impression that you are not really immersed in the [revolutionary] process. There will be a general secretariat with its general secretary, whom you have known for four years--General Torrijos and all the colonels.[17]

Torrijos charged that proposals designed to alter the corporatist structure were "counterrevolutionary," intended "to undermine the total philosophy of the revolution."[18] With that, the NACR proceeded to approve all remaining articles dealing with legislative functions.

Electing the President. The assembly took a break from its struggles to gain new powers in order to exercise one mandate it did possess--electing the president and vice president of the Republic. This was not a routine exercise, since there was someone bold enough to consider running even though his candidacy had not been sanctioned by Torrijos.

That someone was Angueto Riera Pinilla, the head of DIGEDECOM, which had played an important role in identifying, selecting, and training many community representative candidates. Riera Pinilla sought to use his position and DIGEDECOM's role to gain the support of many of the representatives when it came to the presidential nomination and election. Torrijos risked losing control of an institution he had created.

But, as Luis Guagnini observed, "[Riera Pinilla] did not understand that power resided, at that moment, in the National Guard and not in the NACR."[19] The chief of staff of the National Guard ordered the ten military zone commanders to deliver the votes of the representatives from their respective jurisdictions. Riera Pinilla's candidacy withered, and on September 15, 1972, the NACR elected as president Basilio Lakas, who had aided Torrijos in gaining preeminence in December 1969. Arturo Sucre was named vice president.[20] On returning to their constituencies, however, some representatives could not explain why there was only one nominee for president.

The Provincial Level: Budgets. The representatives next attempted to enhance their power at the provincial level, particularly regarding control over the politically sensitive subject of the government budget.

The institutional expression of the people-government administration at the provincial level was the provincial coordinating council. Its membership included the governor and chief of the military zone; the heads of all autonomous and semiautonomous agencies; all heads of provincial branches of national ministries; a representative of the Ministry of Economic Policy, which had no provincial branches; and the representatives. The representatives sat on "working commissions" and the officials sat on "technical commissions."[21]

Article 206 of the draft constitution assigned a number of functions to the provincial coordinating council, among them to promote, coordinate, and conciliate official government activities, and to serve as an organ of consultation. Obviously, Torrijos and members of the Commission on Constitutional Reforms saw competition among government agencies, duplication of effort, and waste of human and material resources as the main problems at the provincial level, problems that the coordinating council should attempt to solve. How this was to take place when provincial-level agencies were only acting on conflicting decisions made by their parent bodies at the national level was never made clear. Also unspecified was the role of the representatives, who were subordinated to the "*technicos*" on the council.

What was clear to some representatives was that the process of drawing up the budget was the heart of politics. Knowing the limits of their power at the national level, where budget formulation was centralized anyway, they sought to maximize their role over spending decisions at the provincial level. Representatives Eliecer Patino and Juvendio Valdes offered an amendment to the draft constitution that would have given the provincial coordination council the power to (1) elaborate the provincial budget on a program-by-program basis; (2) take the legislative initiative in accordance with the second part of Article 150 (which stated the provincial coordinating council may propose legislation through the NACR president, who sat on the CNL); and (3) coordinate all state and local resources. Most significantly, Patino-Valdes proposed that within the council, *the budget be formulated by the representatives and not the technicians, bureaucrats, and military-zone chiefs*.

Defending his proposal, Patino said that planning and budgeting should begin at the bottom and flow to the top, and not the other way around as was then the case. He found it inconceivable that bureaucrats could, from the comfort of their refrigerated offices, draw up plans for communities of which they had no knowledge.[22]

As if to demonstrate the seriousness of the regime's concern regarding Patino-Valdes's amendment, Torrijos himself was present during the debate on it. One of his surrogates, Cocle governor Antonio Jaramillo, said that it was necessary to invite the general to participate because a major change in the state structure was at stake.[23]

NLC Commissioner Ricardo Rodriguez criticized the proposal on the grounds that it misconceived the role of the provincial coordination councils. "The coordinating functions of the council," he said, "were those of discussion, criticism, support, and promotion by representatives of programs presented by the State. The function of the council is not to coordinate state or community resources." For it to do so would "affect one of the pillars of the State as constructed by Torrijos." Rodriguez predicted that if the councils did coordinate state resources, there would be inevitable quarrels among the provinces.[24]

Then Torrijos took up the challenge. He reminded the NACR that if he were to have the powers to implement the nationalist development policies, then he could not afford to have the representatives use the budget-making power to speed up the redistribution of the nation's wealth. To his mind, that would not solve Panama's economic problem: "We are not going to take from the man who has two cows and give to the man who has one cow. Both will end up being poor. We are no enemy of riches. We are enemies of poverty."[25]

Torrijos reassured the NACR that the revolution needed both perspective and faith. Military officers and government officials were to provide the perspective and the representatives the faith. Yet the general was not above materially encouraging that faith: from a special fund he allocated $100,000 for each provincial council to be programmed and spent exclusively by the representatives. He would not allow institutional limits on his power, but he understood the representatives' need to have the wherewithal to reinforce their political credibility in their local communities and their loyalty to their *jefe*.

The Municipality Level: Revenues. In considering the draft constitution's provisions on the municipality level, the representatives focused on the issue of tax revenues. If municipal governments were to play their assigned role in administering and coordinating the central government's development plans and in initiating and implementing plans of its own--particularly small- to medium-scale agricultural and industrial projects, then increased resources would be necessary.

Article 220 of the draft constitution stipulated eight sources of municipal revenues: commodity and land resource taxes; fees from municipal goods and services; fees from public spectacles; profits from the sale of alcoholic beverages; taxes on sand, rocks, clay, and so on; municipal fines; taxes on income from the exploitation of the forest; and income from the national government.[26]

On the first day of debate on municipal governments, a representative proposed to augment their resources by instituting a slaughter tax, a tourist tax, and a Free Zone tax. Caught by surprise, the NLC commissioners asked to have the proposal tabled until the following day, pending consultation with the regime's tax experts.

When debate resumed, Torrijos himself argued against the amendment by elucidating its negative consequences: "Let us not, out of a desire to benefit the municipality, harm a national development plan on which we all agree."[27] A tourist tax would hinder tourism, which attracted a good deal of foreign capital and provided much-needed foreign exchange. A tax on the goods produced in the Colon Free Zone would be a negative signal to foreign companies and foreign capital, and might cost up to 5,000 jobs. With these arguments, the general and the ministers of treasury, agriculture, tourism, and planning were able to convince the proponents of the tourist tax and the Free Zone tax to withdraw the proposals.

There remained the issue of the slaughter tax and which units of government should benefit from it. Traditionally, the tax was assessed where the cattle and pigs were slaughtered, in houses located near urban consumers. The revenues collected were shared by those cities (Colon, Panama, and Chorrera) and the national government, which used a portion for capital improvement in the cattle areas. Representatives from the provinces of Los Santos, Herrera, and Veraguas, which accounted for about half of the cattle raised in the country, claimed that their municipalities should receive and control the slaughter tax revenues.[28]

The government was caught in the conflict of its competing economic policies. On the one hand, it was devoted to a policy of rapid growth in the export sector, through state enterprises, the import of foreign capital, and the long-term stimulation of local-level enterprises producing nontraditional exports. That strategy required centralization for the allocation of limited resources according to a national plan. On the other hand, the regime was committed--at least rhetorically--to job creation, income redistribution, and more equitable balance between regions of the country. This was to be accomplished through the development of small- and medium-sized industries, mostly in rural communities and not necessarily for export. This latter approach implied a high degree of initiative at the municipal level, with the full participation of the representatives.

The regime chose to play on the divisions within the NACR, while protecting its own interests. With NLC commissioners working behind the scenes, an amendment that would have given the municipalities total control over the slaughter tax revenues was defeated. Then the government fought off an effort by Roberto Pinzon and Hoo Mojica, representatives from cattle-grazing districts, to mandate allocation of the revenues to those districts for the exclusive purpose of developing that sector.

NLC commissioners then maneuvered the introduction of an amendment that required the payment of the slaughter tax in the municipality in which the animal was raised.[29] The implication was that the producing districts, not the districts in which the animals were slaughtered, would share the revenues with the national government. As a result, the cleavages within the assembly shifted. It was no longer a conflict between the representatives and the government, or between the owners of cattle ranches and non-owners. It was now the rural representatives, led by Carlos Espino of Los Santos, pitted against their urban counterparts, led by Dr. Walter Lawson of northern Colon. After a brief debate, the amendment was passed.

The victory of the rural municipalities was in some sense symbolic, for the resources that they gained in the slaughter tax revenues were minor relative to the development needs. As in the debate over provincial budgets, Torrijos saw the need to sweeten the pot. He began a program of grants and loans to municipalities to encourage joint economic projects with private enterprises. It was a small price to pay for maintaining control over the national tax base.

<u>Social Justice: The Rights of Labor</u>. Although the regime was populist in its orientation and advocated social justice, it still believed that there was a linkage between social peace, foreign investment, and the success of its development objectives. Torrijos once said that he did not see eye to eye with the deceased Father Hector Gallegos (see chapter 3), because the

priest wanted to make a revolution in his area of Veraguas at 100 miles an hour, while the general wanted to make a revolution at 5 miles an hour, but a revolution that would cover the entire nation. Fearing that too great a velocity would undermine social peace, Torrijos had to make sure that the NACR representatives did not introduce any modifications in the constitution that would increase the rate of social change.

Proposals to guarantee workers' rights to participate in profit sharing threatened to do just that. They again demonstrated the cleavages that divided the assembly. In this case, spokespersons for medium-scale farmers united with defenders of transnational business against those who spoke out for poor workers in both rural and urban areas.

Dolores Miranda Pizarro, who included many workers of the Chiriqui Land Company among his constituents, introduced an amendment to Article 60, which read, "Any worker employed by the State, public or private enterprise, or private individual is guaranteed a minimum wage or salary and the right to share in the profits of mixed or private enterprise; the law will codify this right."[30] The proposal was ardently supported by Fernando Guillen, the representative of banana workers in Bocas del Toro, and by delegates from the latifundia areas of Chiriqui and Veraguas. One supporter explained his view with reference to the story of a retired herdsman who had worked for a cattle rancher for thirty years. The herdsman started with the rancher when the latter had only four head of cattle, and watched his estate grow to 4,000 head and 30,000 hectares of land. The herdsman, however, had nothing to show for his labors.[31]

The majority of representatives from Los Santos and Herrera vehemently opposed the amendment. They feared that the medium-sized farmers they represented would be forced to share their profits with the migrant workers they employed. Other opponents said that workers needed more education and training to increase their productivity before they deserved to share in profits. They argued that Torrijos had already provided workers with many benefits. Carlos Espino of Los Santos labeled the proposal as anticapital and predicted that it would create problems for the revolution and General Torrijos.[32]

The tensions in the NACR were real and obvious. NLC commissioner Ricardo Rodriguez attempted a compromise. He proposed that the provision read, "Only those workers in enterprises designated by law will participate in profit sharing, according to the country's economic condition."[33] His rationale was that profit sharing might reduce investment and production, and would also affect small producers. Dario Pitti supported Rodriguez, saying that it was necessary to postpone profit sharing in order to keep small and medium farmers from becoming allies of the agrocommercial oligarchy. Moreover, "Although the working class has a right to share in the profits of capital," he said, "the principle should not be applied mechanically and in a sectarian manner. It should, rather, be applied dialectically and revolutionarily."[34]

Fernando Guillen offered a countercompromise, which he claimed was a dialectical application of the principle that workers had the right to a share of their employers' profits. He proposed that all workers in public and private enterprises with an annual net profit of over $1 million share 10 percent of the profits. Guillen hoped that his idea would allay the fears of small and medium producers, win the support of representatives close to the Communist party, and gain the regime's favor.

Opposition to the Guillen proposal came from an unexpected quarter. Dr. Walter Lawson, who represented Colon and probably the poorest urban group in Panama, repeated the argument that Torrijos had already provided sufficient benefits to workers, and that profit sharing would precipitate a flight of private capital. Guillen was moved to ask whether Lawson was representing the workers or companies in the $2 billion export enclave. "Sometimes I think this is an Assembly of the CONEP," he quipped.[35]

The first meeting of the NACR and its debates over the new constitution demonstrated the potential and the limits of the corporate populist state. The Torrijos regime was serious about seeing peasants and workers represented in the political system in unprecedented ways. On the other hand, the government did not wish to give up the essential power and flexibility it thought it needed to facilitate economic development and conduct foreign affairs. That conclusion was only reinforced during the 1973 and 1974 sessions of the NACR.

The 1973 NACR Session

<u>Expanding Power: Failure Anew</u>. As representatives assembled in October 1973, many believed that the system of consultation in which General Torrijos had placed so much stock had not worked well. They claimed that the NACR president did not keep members informed, and that the NACR's companion legislative body, the CNL, enacted

laws without consultation with it or, in some cases, the provincial coordination councils.

As a result, there were recommendations to change the assembly's internal rules to provide for three types of consultation: provincial consultation, joint consultation, and national consultation. National consultation was of grave concern to Torrijos because it would have given the NACR the power to call full plenary meetings on any question it wished. The general felt that this recommendation threatened an important executive prerogative.

He therefore called a meeting of key NACR members and the NLC. He pressured the representatives to withdraw the proposal, and they soon complied. Another NACR attempt to assert some influence over the legislative and decision-making process was denied. About the only channel left to the representatives was the passage of resolutions that expressed the concerns and aspirations of a majority of the assembly. For the regime, resolutions had the advantage of not having legal standing: the government had great flexibility in deciding whether and how to respond to them.[36]

<u>Opposing the Oligarchy: Following Torrijos's Lead</u>. The year 1973 saw an intensification of tensions between Torrijos and the displaced oligarchy. The latter sought to stop the leftward movement of the regime and even tried to destabilize it.

The first conflict was in the province of Chiriqui, where Torrijos had appointed Ornel Urriola, a member of the Party of the People, as governor, and where the FEP was attempting to push a leftist reform of the educational system. In July and August the oligarchy responded by mounting a series of demonstrations called the "<u>Chiricanazo</u>" (see Chapter 4).

The second issue was housing. The government had drafted a new housing code, which called for subsidized public housing and forms of rent control, and reorganized the housing agency into a Ministry of Housing. The landlords and the Panama Construction Association opposed the new housing bill, particularly the provisions concerning subsidies and rent control, and a prohibition on eviction for nonpayment of rent. CONEP threatened to hold a strike on October 15th to express its opposition to the housing legislation.

The NACR quickly sprang to Torrijos's defense. It passed a resolution condemning the <u>Chiricanazo</u> and the CONEP threat, and praised the housing bill and the 1925

Tenants' Movement. The resolution suggested that the actions of the oligarchy were as destabilizing as steps taken by the right wing in Chile before the overthrow of Allende.

The unanimity with which the representatives acted was quickly shattered by another resolution condemning the leading families of the oligarchy and calling for the removal of their names from public places, buildings, and streets. Names like Rodrigo Chiari, Mario Calindo, Archibaldo Boyd, Ricardo Arango, Mario de Diego, Eduardo Chiari, and Horacio Alfaro were to be replaced by those of "people's heroes"--such as Marciano Mirones, Ferdin Jaen, Lorenzo Brown, Emilio Olivardia, Damian Cabrera, Julian Camarena, and Antonio Landazo.[37]

The resolution was initially approved but was called to the assembly floor the next day for reconsideration. Speaking for reconsideration were Eberto Anguizola, a representative from Chiriqui and a former Arias supporter; Benjamin Quintero, a medium-scale sugar producer from Herrera; and, strangely enough, Cocle governor Antonio Jaramillo, the most loyal supporter of Torrijos in the NACR. They criticized the resolution for damaging the prestige of prominent families, for fostering negative consequences for the revolution, and for responding to the "parasitic" and "opportunistic" policies of the Communist party.

Dario Pitti, a communist labor leader from Chiriqui, defended the resolution, for he understood well its symbolic and ideological effect. As he put it, "Last night was certainly a night of distress for the oligarchy. Yesterday a resolution was approved here which definitively eliminated its past political representatives, its figures, as worthy of having a place of honor as social and political representatives."[38] Pitti warned the NACR that a vote for reconsideration was a vote of concession to the oligarchy and reminded his colleagues that Torrijos was also anti-oligarchy. But his oratory failed, and the motion to reconsider was approved.[39]

Thus the NACR demonstrated that it did not wish to push its anti-oligarchy views too far on its own. Out of fear of antagonizing the old elite, the government may have been working to restrain assembly (Torrijos himself reversed his appointment of Urriola). In addition, patrimonial social relations still existed in many rural communities, and many representatives may have been influenced by clientelist relations with patrons in the oligarchy.

Next it was the right wing's turn to overstep itself. Conservative elements in the assembly--especially Anguizola--moved to condemn the FEP and the Party of the People for attempting to use educational reforms to entrench themselves in government positions and for their role in provoking the Chiricanazo. To preserve the delicate balance between left and right, Minister of Justice Materno Vasquez admonished Anguizola, saying that the Communist party, like all other parties and their spokespersons, was free to express opinions as long as it did not subvert Torrijos or the revolutionary regime. The resolution went no further. Nevertheless, the Chiricanazo incident had strengthened the right-wing elements in the NACR and weakened the progressive forces.

The 1974 NACR Session

The Economic Crisis: Labor's Deteriorating Position. When the assembly reconvened in October 1974 for its third session, the recession had significantly deepened and inflation was continuing its dizzy spiral. The political fallout was a struggle over who would bear the burden of bad times and who was best able to pull the country out of the crisis. The business and latifundia interests appealed for better treatment than they had gotten since 1968, and Torrijos was tailoring economic policies to be at least somewhat responsive (his Boquete Declaration was only a month away). The representatives tended to take the side of the poor, charging that speculators were victimizing peasants, workers, and consumers in general, and that the government's Office of Price Control was ineffective in stopping them.

Yet the 1974 session of the NACR was divided on one of the major issues of the day, the 1972 labor code.[40] Although the Party of the People and other allies of urban workers supported the code, those who represented small- and medium-scale producers--especially delegates from Los Santos and Herrera--were convinced that the law worked against the interests of their constituencies.

One of those was Representative Matias Cedeno. He chose not to attack the code itself, because that would only be seen as support for CONEP's calls for major modification or abrogation of the law. Instead, Cedeno made a case against the way the code was being implemented. He claimed that small-scale farmers were unaware of their rights and duties under the statute, and that its application was detrimental to them. Cedeno cited a case where a poultry producer was compelled to give vacation and notification pay to a worker dismissed for using eggs to play baseball.[41]

The regime was in a dilemma: the labor code was the basis for labor's membership in the populist alliance, but the government could not afford to alienate private enterprise during such a crisis. Particularly in the NACR, where the voice of the rural petty bourgeoisie was clearly heard, it was difficult to mobilize sympathy for the many workers who were out on strike. Torrijos knew this, and he acted as if both workers and capitalists were equally at fault for the slowdown in the economy (when in fact several major companies provoked strikes by dismissing laborers). Torrijos demonstrated particular annoyance at workers for the shutdown of Citrico-Chiriqui, S.A., which the government took over after mediation failed. As Torrijos told the assembly:

> I am also telling the workers not to get carried away by false union gains. These are oftentimes illusory because neither business, businessmen, nor salaried workers can sustain those gains. Lately I witnessed such a case of excessive gains which could not be sustained by Citrico-Chiriqui.[42]

Thus Torrijos's position was moving toward that of CONEP and rural small- and medium-scale producers. Application of the code would soon be relaxed and three years later it would be amended. Labor's ability to defend its interests was quite limited and the Party of the People recognized its relative lack of influence. As one of its journals concluded: "If it is true that the worker-peasant alliance provides a measure of support to the government, it is certainly not a factor in the government's decision-making."[43] But the government had less reason to take the worker-peasant alliance into account when it was deeply divided, as the debates in the NACR all too readily demonstrated.

The Canal Zone Negotiations: True Believers. In the latter part of 1974, anxieties also grew about the failure of rapid progress on the negotiations with the United States. The eight-point agreement of principles concluded by Secretary of State Kissinger and Foreign Minister Tack had been a political victory, since the United States had agreed to abolish the 1903 treaty. But nationalists inside and outside of the government had found other elements of the agreement disturbing, and the Watergate crisis had brought negotiations to a standstill. In response, the organizations that made up the popular alliance, particularly the Party of the People, defended Torrijos and the Tack-Kissinger agreement.

NACR representatives themselves were generally not attuned to the canal issue. Very few of the fifty representatives interviewed in 1974 (most of whom were from rural communities outside the transit area) knew what the Tack-Kissinger agreements were. Most expressed concern about the amount of money Panama had received from the United States for the use of the canal and the Zone. Some felt Panama should be given more money but that U.S. interests should be ensured. A minority, most of whom were from areas close to the Zone, called for the immediate evacuation of the U.S. military and civilian institutions.[44] All informants expressed confidence that General Torrijos would not betray them and that he would negotiate a nationalist treaty.

In defending the government's position, Foreign Minister Tack told the NACR that the United States could not be asked to abandon Panama militarily anytime soon, and that Panama would insist on a certain date for the end of the U.S. military presence in the Canal Zone and the nation. Although the United States was still demanding control over the canal for forty to fifty years, it was clear that Panama was willing to allow some U.S. military presence for another twenty-five years.

Only one person had questions for the foreign minister--Representative Luis Veces, a lawyer, a Christian Democrat, and an opponent of the regime. He asked:

--whether it was true that NLC commissioners were negotiating the treaty rather than the foreign minister (that was later shown to be the case).

--why Panama was proposing to legalize the U.S. military bases.

--what Panama was gaining in return for such a concession.

--why the National Guard had set up an office in the Canal Zone to cooperate with the U.S. Southern Command.

Veces also rejected the government's position that it had only three courses of action--do nothing, conduct armed struggle, and negotiate a possible treaty. Veces claimed that Panama had exercised another alternative in 1926, 1947, and 1967: rejected treaties not in the national interest.

Finally, Veces insisted that Minister Tack detail the negotiating process to the NACR. There was an immediate reaction from Representative Jaramillo, governor of Cocle and a Torrijos loyalist. He invoked the Nation's security as the reason why Tack should not be obliged to answer. Jaramillo said that many representatives could not be trusted with that sort of detailed information, and that furthermore there were probably CIA agents in the audience. It was suggested that Tack meet with some representatives in closed session. With that, the session ended. With the sole exception of Veces, the NACR demonstrated full confidence in Torrijos and was willing to follow his lead rather than share in the making of foreign policy.

Faltering Prestige. Two incidents during the 1974 session brought home the limits of the NACR's power and esteem. Many representatives from the interior provinces decided to lodge at the National Gymnasium, the site of the assembly's sessions, in order to save the twenty-dollar-per-day stipend. A porter ordered them to mop the floor where they were to sleep. The representatives were outraged and brought the matter to the NACR, and the body asked that action be taken against the porter or his ultimate superior, the minister of sports and culture.

The assembly ordered Minister Altamirano Duque to appear before it. (Duque was a member of one of the traditional rich Panamanian families with controlling interest in the National Brewery, newspapers, and insurance companies.) The representatives found Duque's manner and answers disrespectful, and passed a resolution calling on General Torrijos to request the resignations of all top bureaucrats and to appoint individuals who could work with the NACR. There was some hope of success, since Torrijos had very recently requested the resignation of all ambassadors and consuls, and the representatives themselves had previously succeeded in getting the general to replace several uncooperative mayors and governors. But for Torrijos to engage in a total housecleaning risked upsetting the delicate balance of power among the National Guard colonels, each of whom had their "team" of clients scattered through the ministries and agencies.

Having failed to wrest more power, the representatives contented themselves with more money. Right before adjournment, Hoo Mojica recommended that the government allocate more funds to the municipalities and the community boards (on which the representatives sat). The national officials, who had made sure that the representatives had no power over the formulation of budgets and no control over any portion of the tax base, were glad to comply. Minister of Planning Barletta revealed that he had just secured a $5 million loan from AID earmarked for municipal development projects. He urged the representatives to plan and program such projects early, for the monies were forthcoming as of June 1974.[45]

The members of the NACR were just what their titles suggested--representatives. Try as some of their number might, they were never able to establish the role of legislator for themselves or to convince the executive to give them some of its powers. On some questions, such as the political status of the oligarchy and the Canal Zone negotiations, the great majority of the delegates were willing to simply exercise the faith that Torrijos asked of them. When the assembly was deeply divided over certain issues (like the labor code), it was more easily manipulated by Torrijos, who in the end was the only person who could resolve major conflicts of interest. Be all that as it may, the fact remains that social groups and classes that were never allowed to participate directly in politics were now able to do so. That in and of itself was an accomplishment.

NOTES

1. The four were leading members of the National Legislative Commission (NLC) and went on to prominent official positions. Royo became minister of education, was one of the principals in the canal negotiations, and in 1978 was Torrijos's hand-picked candidate for president. Rodriguez became minister of government and justice. Ahumada served as minister of labor, and Jaen became president of the NLC.

2. Rodriguez spoke on radio on October 11, 1973, the fifth anniversary of the revolution.

3. For a theoretical treatment of how populist states defend and at the same time limit the rights of peasants, blacks, Indians, and workers, see Roger Bartra, "La Mediacion Democratica y la Democracia sin Medicacion," _Estudios Sociales Centroamericanos_, no. 16 (1977).

4. Luis Guagnini, "Model Panameno: La Estructura de Poder in Panama y el Balance entre la Izquierda y la Derecha," _Tareas_, no. 32 (1975), p. 14.

5. The term ultra-left in this context was used by the regime to describe all the independent Left organizations that had refused to subordinate themselves to it.

6. For an official version of how the system should function, see Miguel Angel Picard-Ami, _Estructura Politica del Poder Popular Panameno_ (Panama, 1975).

7. See Articles 2 and 277 of the 1972 constitution of the Republic of Panama.

8. Ibid.

9. Based on interviews with DIGEDECOM officials in Panama City in May 1974; on interviews with fifty representatives in 1974; and on _Memoria_ of DIGEDECOM for the years 1972 and 1973. Pages 30-82 of the 1972 edition has detailed, province-by-province reports on the operations and training of personnel. Of course, some representatives had needed no encouragement to run for office. Some of them, the one from El Coco in Penonome, Cocle, for example, was critical of DIGEDECOM's role, because of its dependence on AID.

10. Renato Pereira, _Panama: Fuerzas Armadas y Politica_ (Panama, 1979), p. 139.

11. _Estrella de Panama_, September 1, 1972.

12. _Matutina_, September 5, 1972.

13. See Republic of Panama, NACR, _Diario de los Debates_ 1 (Panama, 1972), p. 17.

14. Ibid., p. 109.

15. Ibid., p. 110.

16. Ibid., p. 127 and p. 138.

17. Ibid., p. 126.

18. Ibid., p. 148.

19. Luis Guagnini, "Model Panameno," pp. 26-27.

20. _Diario de los Debates_ 1 (1972), p. 188.

21. _Estrella de Panama_, September 27, 1972.

22. _Diario de los Debates_ 2 (1972), p. 410.

23. Ibid., p. 397.

24. Ibid., p. 410.

25. Ibid.

26. _Constitucion Politica de la Republica de Panama_ (1972), p. 77.

27. _Diario de los Debates_ 2 (1972), p. 439.

28. According to the 1970 agricultural census, there were 1,259,892 head of cattle in Panama on May 16, 1971--376,655 head in Chiriqui, 128,828 in Herrera, 275,559 in Los Santos, 212,881 in Veraguas, and only 19,478 in Colon and 130,918 in Panama. _Censos Nacionales de 1970, III Censo Agropecuarion (16 de Mayo de 1971) Vol II Produccion Pecuaria_ (Panama), pp. 16-18.

29. _Diario de los Debates_ 2 (1972), p. 440.

30. Ibid., p. 234.

31. Ibid.

32. Ibid., p. 239.

33. Ibid., p. 237.

34. Ibid.

35. Ibid., p. 301.

36. The process for handling resolutions was explained to the NACR by the NLC's Miguel Angel Picard-Ami. See _Diario de los Debates_ 3 (1974), p. 630.

37. _Diario de los Debates_ 2 (1973), pp. 453-58.

38. Ibid., p. 469.

39. Ibid., p. 470. For Torrijos's views on the oligarchy, see his "La Oligarquia no tiene Nacionalidad," _Tareas_, no. 39.

40. Among other things, the labor code provided for compulsory unionization, job security, paid vacation, and so on.

41. _Diario de los Debates_ 1 (1974), p. 308.

42. Ibid., p. 49.

43. "Sobre la Situacion Panamena," _Sintesis_ 1 (Dec. 1977):22.

44. Because representatives from neither Colon nor Panama City were interviewed, it was not possible to obtain what might have been a more militant and nationalist position on the canal question. The impact of that deficiency is not great, however, because those two cities were underrepresented in the NACR.

45. _Diario de los Debates_ 3 (1974), p. 700.

6

Local Participatory Structures: The Community Boards

The preceding chapter described the process by which a role was defined for the representatives in the national political system. In that arena, the representatives were frustrated by a military regime that was reluctant to grant them decision-making powers even as it mobilized their support. To the extent that the representatives exercised influence, it was in reflecting the interests of the nation's contending social forces. This chapter relates the role of the representative in the local political system, particularly in the rural areas and particularly in attempting to foster economic development. In that context, representatives tended to be more effective when they had support from the officials in the national government and when they did not face obstacles from local vested interests.

The Legal and Political Context of Community Boards

The formation of community boards (*juntas comunales*) was provided for in the 1972 constitution: "Every corregimiento (505) is to have a Junta Comunal which would promote the collective development, solve problems and conciliate local differences."[1] The 1972 constitution defined the functions of the representatives as follows: parole officer, evaluator of teacher performance, watchdog of bureaucracies, economic catalyst, and community organizer.

By 1973 Law 105, which regulated the functioning of the community boards, had been drawn up by the National Legislative Commission (NLC), approved by the National Legislative Council (CNL), presented to each of the nine provincial coordination councils, and finally modified and ratified by the National Assembly of Community Representatives (NACR). The nucleus of each community board was the traditional appointed *corregidor* and an elected community representative (*representante*).[2] In addition, three community residents, invariably chosen by the representative, sat on each board.[3]

In general terms, Law 105 conceived of the community boards as part of the state machinery whose function it was to implement, at the local level, all government policies and at the same time channel all demands from local community groups (*juntas locales*) to the top. They were to be transmission belts for programs devised in the bureaucracy and organs of mediation and conciliation at the local level. In practice, the community boards also served as political channels for grass-roots support for the Torrijos regime, as mechanisms for implementing governmental redistributive and economic and economic programs at the local level, and as "watchdogs" of the bureaucracy.

There was a distinct difference in the objectives pursued by urban community boards and those in the rural areas. In the urban areas, the economic problems--inflation, unemployment--were too severe to be solved with the resources available to the boards. As a result, they did not transcend the *corregidor's* traditional coercive role of local judge and law enforcer.[4] In the rural area, there was more room for local initiative in addressing poverty.

Yet the community boards in rural areas could not exercise this initiative without support from government institutions outside their local areas. Representatives found it difficult to carry out many of their functions if *corregidores*, municipal mayors, and provincial governors were uncooperative. The representative had to be in contact with bureaucrats from autonomous agencies and ministries. They continued to deal with DIGEDECOM officials, who organized many of the boards and continued to provide periodic community training. Additionally, representatives experienced a substantial amount of interaction with AID bureaucrats, since the training programs were financed with AID funds.

The most important point of contact for the community boards in the national government was the National Legislative Commission. As the successor to the Commission on Constitutional Reforms, which wrote into the constitution the idea of political participation at all levels by representatives, the NLC served as the boards' political ideologist, as their economic advisor, and as their advocate with the bureaucracy. The relationship between the community boards and the NLC was a vertical one within the populist-corporatist state. The representative, presiding over the board, had important economic, political, and ombudsman functions within the community. But in order to carry out these functions, the representative had to rely heavily on the NLC--both economically and politically.

As ideologists of the new system, NLC members wrote pamphlets to explain how the system should work, gave lectures, and led discussions for bureaucrats. Most importantly they made periodic trips to the corregimientos to monitor the progress of economic projects and to give suggestions to the representatives on how to solve social or political problems. Whenever the local bureaucracy or military failed to support the community board, the representative could appeal directly to the NLC and Torrijos himself.[5] When appropriate, the representatives would enlist the support of the NLC to remove such uncooperative officials.[6] In effect, the relationship between the NLC and the community boards provided the populist-corporatist structure with the flexibility it needed in order to function.

The NLC held both sticks and carrots in sustaining that relationship. The stick was the NLC's control over legislation that had the potential of threatening the incumbency of the sitting representatives. One of the NLC's responsibilities was to initiate legislation to bring into effect procedures set forth in the constitution. One of these was the "recall mandate" ("revocatoria de mandato"),[7] by which a constituency could remove its representative. Because many delegates were elected with as little as 25 percent of the vote,[8] they recognized full well that they were politically vulnerable. The NLC knew that by refraining from drawing up legislation to implement the constitutionally mandated right of recall, it held a club over the representatives, a way of keeping the representatives in line with government programs and policies.[9]

Being protected by the NLC from community recall had its price. As Carlos Espino of Los Santos (1973 NACR president) indicated, most representatives liked the fact that the NLC refrained from allowing the implementation of the recall mandate. Yet many, such as Feliciana Grajales of San Isidro in San Miguelito, complained that members of the NLC incited the community against the representatives so as to weaken their power and authority.[10]

The carrot was money. Each community board was entitled to a yearly minimum grant of $1000 from General Torrijos. Although the representatives generally appreciated the concept of the grant, many of those who did receive it found it insufficient. Those who, for budgetary reasons, did not receive any grant were discontented. Thus Planning Minister Barletta had to promise that representatives who received no money in 1974 would have priority in 1975.

In addition to the grants, the community boards depended on several loans fought for by the NLC, approved by the minister of economic policy and planning, financed by AID, and disbursed by the National Bank. For the year 1974-75, the Ministry of Economic Policy and Planning borrowed from AID a sum of $5 million at a rate of 3 percent for forty years. These funds were to be used by the community boards and municipalities for what Minister of Planning Barletta called "productive investments," the main objective being the creation of jobs.[11] Barletta was also able to negotiate an additional sum of $20.4 million: $8.8 million from AID for cooperative ventures and the balance from the Inter-American Development Bank (BID) for agricultural credits and small-scale fishing. These funds were intended for local use by local entities.

Funds for local projects were not exclusively provided by public international lending agencies. Barletta also obtained loans from foreign private banks with branches in Panama. For example, the $5 million that was promised to the community boards for the fiscal year 1975 was expected to be late, so Barletta obtained an advance from the Bank of Tokyo. He also negotiated and received an additional $7 million from locally based foreign banks to be channeled through the Agricultural Development Bank (BDA) for agricultural credits.[12]

There were representatives who believed that the benefit of monetary resources provided from above was outweighed by the accompanying dependency. Many felt that financing could be generated for road building, school construction, etc., if such projects were carried out through the community boards rather than through the national ministries.[13] For them, the issue was not whether or not they could build schools and roads at lower costs than the national ministries (and the community boards argued forcibly that they could). It was whether or not the government was willing to decentralize some of the infrastructural work for national modernization by allowing the community boards to design and construct portions of these projects. They hoped to increase their control over monies obtained from Torrijos and administered by the NLC.

The Community Boards and the Health Committees

One of the functions of the community boards was to

coordinate the efforts of all local groups. To ensure the cooperation of these groups, all government funds channeled into the community went through the community board. Just as the regime at the national level had subordinated all popular structures and movements, the community boards also moved swiftly, with the help of the regime, to subordinate all existing local structures--in particular the health committees (*comites de salud*).[14]

In 1974 there were at least 800 health committees in more than 500 *corregimientos*. Created in December 1970 by Decree Law 401, they represented the most democratic participatory structure at that moment. The slogan "Equal Health for All" ("*Salud Igual Para Todos*"), coined by the regime, was taken seriously in those communities where health committees were organized. But the concentration of income and physical resources in the capital city and an exploitative land tenure system made it difficult, if not impossible, for the urban and especially the rural masses to gain access to enough food, water, land, toilets, or health facilities to make "equal health for all" a reality.

The health committees represented the hopes of many in these communities to gain access to these services. But more importantly, the health committees encouraged full, active, and aggressive participation in the local communities. This kind of participation oftentimes clashed with local established interests, especially in the rural communities.

The committees were organized by the Ministry of Health and therefore represented a potential power base that could be used by political forces not entirely committed to Torrijos. The Riera Pinilla case had taught the regime a good lesson (Pinilla had attempted to use his position as director of DIGEDECOM to get himself elected president of the Republic by the NACR).

Consequently, several steps were taken to ensure that the well-organized health committees would not constitute an autonomous community-based organization. First, in discussing their role during the constitutional reforms, Commissioner Adolfo Ahumada (later minister of labor) made it clear that to mention the health committees by name within the constitution would be tantamount to giving them equal local jurisdiction with the community boards. They were not mentioned. Secondly, the minister of health, Dr. Renan Esquivel,[15] was removed and replaced by Dr. Abraham Saied, Torrijos's brother-in-law. Thirdly, within the Ministry of Health there were several personnel changes and structural reforms, weakening the support systems of the health committees. Lastly, at the local level the community boards either took control of the health committees, frustrated their many functions, or ignored them.[16]

As of 1974 the problems between the community boards and the health committees were far from being solved. Not only was this indicated in interviews with representatives in 1974, but in the 1974 NACR session, outgoing president Carlos Espino challenged the new minister of health, Abraham Saied:

> I [Espino] would like Minister Saied to explain to us the policies of the Health Committees, and to inform us as to whether they are subordinated to the functions of the Junta Comunal, for the strengthening of the revolutionary system to which we all belong. . . . The Health Committees are very organized and they should recognize the legal standing of the Junta Comunal.[17]

Economic Enterprises

The economic function of the community boards was to design and implement agricultural and industrial projects that would create permanent employment sufficient to bring stability to the rural communities. As of June 1974 only ninety-eight representatives, in consultation with the NLC, had designed projects, most of which were small-scale agricultural, cattle, or poultry projects. The projects took various forms. In some the community board used its money to form mixed enterprises with private capital. In others the board used its funds to purchase land, which was to become the foundation of the project. In yet others, the board secured contracts from the national government.

But the economic tasks of the community boards were made difficult by their limited resources and the frequently hostile context in which they functioned. Although funding for the projects came from a variety of sources, most communities could only count on the $1000 given by Torrijos (and in some cases that was not completely certain). Agrarian reform had left intact the economic and social power of the oligarchy, so it was often difficult for the boards to secure land (since all the good acreage was already in private hands). They also found it hard to counter the harassment and sabotage of those whose economic interests were threatened, and sometimes the obstruction of government officials. These obstacles are best demonstrated by citing several case studies.

Mixed Enterprises. One of the great hopes for the success of the community boards was their efforts to form profitable mixed enterprises with private capital. Of the ninety-eight early community projects submitted to the NLC, only three were of this nature: a slaughter-house, a handkerchief factory, and a clothing factory.

The Los Santos slaughterhouse was a mixed enterprise of local agribusiness and seven municipalities of Los Santos. In 1974 the representatives of each of the municipalities agreed to financially support the project, a decision that grew out of the NACR discussion of the slaughter tax in 1972 (see Chapter 5). The estimated cost of the project was $1.15 million, of which the cattle owners agreed to invest $105,000, with the balance to be borrowed by the municipalities. The municipalities, as we have seen, needed the prior approval of the national government before obtaining loans. In most cases, moreover, the loan would have to be guaranteed by the national government.

Mr. Miguel Sanchiz, the minister of the treasury at the time, was considered an expert on the financing of slaughterhouses, an expertise he developed during his earlier years with the Chase Manhattan Bank. He refused to guarantee the loan, claiming that the project would run into severe competition from existing facilities and would therefore not be profitable.

The representatives from Los Santos had convinced Torrijos and a majority of the members of the CNL of the feasibility and desirability of the project. Both Torrijos and the CNL had approved it. Minister Sanchiz dissented from the majority and was able to exercise a temporary veto on the project by convincing Torrijos that the terms of the loan were highly unfavorable.[18]

The Los Santos loan was for eight years and Sanchiz believed that it could not be repaid within that period of time. The government, acting as loan guarantor, would be responsible for repaying if Los Santos defaulted. (Chiriqui had just defaulted on a similar $1.7 million loan.)

The loan for the slaughterhouse was eventually approved because it had the active support of important local landlords and all the representatives of the province. However, for a short period of time, Sanchiz had been able to successfully block what all these representatives considered the province's most important economic project.[19]

The handkerchief factory in Guarare suffered a different fate. This mixed enterprise, undertaken by the joint efforts of the community board, AID, and community women, was initiated by Abdiel Perez of the corregimiento of Guarare in Los Santos. He obtained a $12,000 building from AID in which the handkerchief factory was housed. But when local merchants became unable to compete with the factory, they pressured Perez to discontinue the project.

He then attempted to organize a joint community board-salt workers project. But this effort failed also, because the small producers of salt, who remained loyal to one Mr. Cohen, refused to do business with the community board. Mr. Cohen, the wholesaler and retailer of salt in the area, was successful in convincing the small producers not to deal with the community board.[20]

The Gualaca clothing factory in Chiriqui was much more successful. Gualaca, a small community about twenty miles west of David, had a very high rate of migration, especially among its young inhabitants. The representative hoped that in setting up the clothing factory, at least the younger women would remain. The cost of the factory was estimated at $25,000, which would be in the form of a loan to the community board by the National Bank. A Colombian manufacturer with fourteen years' experience in New York contributed expertise and an undisclosed supply of material imported from New York. The Colombian obtained a minority share of the enterprise, tax-free importation of the materials, and a managerial position in the factory. The community board employed fifty-two women, and at the moment was partially successful in ameliorating its migration and unemployment difficulties.

The community boards, therefore, faced many complex problems as they attempted to set up economic enterprises that either cost too much or were too competitive for local merchants or landlords. When these two factors did not come into play, the community boards were apparently able to set up mixed enterprises with some measure of success.

Land Acquisition. Most community boards situated in either of the terminal cities or near a large estate or private or foreign enterprise usually found it difficult to establish viable economic enterprises. In most cases, attracting workers was a difficult task in itself, because workers tended to seek what they perceived as more stable or higher-paying jobs with the larger, more established enterprises. In other cases, there was not enough land for agricultural projects. So most rural dwellers either migrated or worked temporarily in the peasant settlements or community board projects while still searching for employment elsewhere, especially with foreign firms.[21]

It was for this reason, therefore, that community boards in such areas tended to try to acquire land in order to create jobs. An examination of four cases (Aguadulce, near the Nestle's factory; Changuinola, near the banana plantation; Villa Rosario in Panama; and Vista Alegre in Colon) will demonstrate the ways in which the representatives went about acquiring land, the difficulties they encountered, and the kinds of help (or lack of help) they received from bureaucrats.

All these communities shared one factor in common: they were relatively well populated due to their proximity to either terminal cities or to large foreign enterprises. Consequently, they all faced a similar problem: securing enough community land to prevent squatting and its political repercussions.

Pocri, Aguadulce, was home to Nestle's processing complex along with the privately owned sugar mills of Estrella and Santa Rosa. This center attracted a large number of migrants who, having no land of their own, squatted on privately owned land. The owners wanted the squatters to either buy the land, at exorbitant prices, or get off.

In order to alleviate the situation, the representative of Pocri decided in 1974 to obtain an extension of community land, parcel it, and sell it to the squatters at reasonable prices and terms of payment. However, the National Department for Agrarian Reform (DINRA) dragged its feet, and the representative could not distribute the land as fast as the situation required. Meanwhile, the conflict between squatters and owners was intensifying. The representative appealed to the director of the land survey, Francisco Sibauste, who promised to consult with DINRA to find a solution.[22] DINRA never found a solution.

The land problem in Changuinola was a little different. The banana company owned the land in practically the entire community, including the graveyard. The municipality and corregimiento had very little space to expand.

In recent years, the banana firm had not absorbed many new workers. The representative, concerned with the long-run viability of the community, often verbally castigated the inhabitants for having a "cash mentality," that is, having no interest in working the land. Using the experience of the peasant settlements in Progreso, Chiriqui (formed from lands turned over to the government by the Chiriqui Land Company) as a model, he hoped to obtain sufficient property from the banana company to set up peasant settlements or other productive units. However, the government would first have to convince the company to release the necessary land. The government in this case did not succeed.

In 1974 the community board of Vista Alegre, district of Arraijan, province of Panama, was just as ineffective when it tried to buy land. Vista Alegre's population as of 1970 was only 2,320. The government, however, had plans to build hundreds of low-cost housing units in the area, and the population was expected to soar to 100,000 in less than ten years. The representative decided that the community board should seek to purchase the land in order to resell it, at a profit, to the Ministry of Housing, or parcel out some land to community members who might want to remain in the area but who could not afford the low-cost housing. But when he investigated purchasing the land, he found that it had been bought up by the Compania Vista Alegre, S.A. The company had bought the land, sold a portion to the Housing and Urbanization Institute (IVU), and kept another portion with which to speculate.[23]

Where the economic stakes were not so high, the community boards tended to have greater opportunities and less competition from private capital. Such was the case in Villa Rosario in the district of Capira, province of Panama. The community was one of large absentee cattle owners, many small cattle ranchers, and a large number of recent migrants from the interior provinces. The latter were squatters in an area called Victoriano Lorenzo.

In order to prevent a situation of social conflict between squatters and owners, the community representative, Mr. Martinez, had a plan. He intended to acquire as much land as possible, parcel it into lots of 20 x 30 meters, then sell the lots at $50 each to the squatters. The land he had his eye on belonged to a latifundista who had died recently. The government was in the process of confiscating the more than fourteen hectares because the owner had been delinquent on the payment of taxes. With the help of Lt. Col. Ruben Dario Paredes, Mr. Martinez was able to obtain the land.

(After Torrijos died in 1981, Paredes became head of the National Guard.)

During the summer of 1974 Mr. Martinez also applied for a loan through the National Bank to purchase another piece of land; however, neither the bank manager, the mayor, the municipal council, nor the representative knew the procedure to obtain the loan. The representative called Marcelino Jaen, the NLC president, who in turn called Mr. Ricardo De La Espriella, the general director of the National Bank, who then ordered the Chorrera branch of the bank to put through the loan. (In 1982 Mr. De La Espriella, with support from General Paredes, assumed the presidency.)

In the above cases the representatives were involved in conciliating disputes between squatters and owners. However, in doing so, we see once more that they were highly dependent on members of the NLC, the military, and bureaucrats of other agencies for assistance in carrying out their responsibilities.

Government Contracts. The government was interested in achieving income redistribution and sectoral balance not only by public spending on education, health, and public works and by encouraging private and mixed enterprise investments, but also by offering government contracts to community boards. Two such cases were to be found in Atalaya, Veraguas, and in the old colonial community of Parita, Herrera.

The Atalaya project was a $77,700 loan obtained through National Bank to purchase two tractors. The tractors were used in preparing forty hectares of land for the cultivation of maize, and rented to the state-owned sugar mill, Ingenio La Victoria, during six months of each year.[24]

In addition, the community board requested a loan of $85,000 to $250,000 for a limestone project. Whether or not it would obtain the loan would depend on a number of economic and political factors. The government might be interested in its import-substitution effect, saving millions of dollars in import costs and its consequent impact on the nation's balance of payments. Moreover, if members of the NLC could be convinced of the feasibility of the project, they might very well intervene and lobby in favor of the loan. The success of the project depended entirely on whether the government would decide to encourage the import substitution of limestone.

In Parita the representative, a young university graduate, organized a training program for high school dropouts. The dropouts were trained to rehabilitate old colonial structures such as temples, altars, churches, or any other colonial structure that the National Foundation (Patronato Nacional) or the National Institute of Culture (INAC) were willing to preserve as historical monuments. The foundation and INAC both advanced thousands of dollars to the community board to rehabilitate various structures. The students received $5.00 a week while they were being trained. Because the heads of these organizations were behind the representative and supported his efforts, this project had an opportunity for a measure of success.[25]

Watchdog Functions

The bureaucracy had long been a source of patronage in Panamanian politics, and under Torrijos patronage continued. The bureaucracy grew from 48,986 to over 84,000 employees between the years 1965 and 1975.[26] With such a large number of people involved, Torrijos recognized that he had to cope with two problems. First, he had to ensure loyalty at the top, and second, he had to ensure performance in the field. The representatives were assigned the task of overseeing the performance of the bureaucracy at the community level.

In the midst of the economic crisis of 1973 and 1974, during which representatives were forced to acknowledge their powerlessness in matters of national policy, they got more mileage out of exposing two major bureaucratic scandals. In one they were ultimately successful; in the other they were not.

The Public Works Case. The Torrijos government had initiated an aggressive road construction program, primarily feeder roads to link rural communities to regional or major arterial roads and markets. The program was centralized in the Ministry of Public Works under Minister Nestor Tomas Guerra. The project was financed largely by the Inter-American Development Bank (BID) under the names of CAM-BID 1, 2, 3, and so on.[27]

By mid-1974 there was pressure from communities through their representatives for the regime to do something about the inefficient performance of the Ministry of Public Works. Sparked in part by Representative Joaquin Espinosa's uncovering of huge discrepancies in what the ministry said it did and what was actually done, the government announced major changes in the CAM-BID program, as well as personnel changes within the ministry.

Representative Espinosa was from Rio Hato in the province of Cocle and was vice president of the NACR in 1974. He also had ready access to Gen. Torrijos, whose military headquarters was located in Rio Hato. Whether or not he consulted with Torrijos before publicly condemning and ridiculing the minister of public works at the 1974 assembly is not known. However, he did consult with dozens of representatives, all of whom gave him detailed descriptions of public works discrepancies as they existed in their respective communities.

As part of the yearly written and oral report given by agencies and bureaucrats to the NACR in session, Minister Guerra claimed an overall 70 percent completion of CAM-BID projects in the province of Cocle. Immediately, Espinosa outlined four projects for which the minister had claimed 100 percent completion, labeling them "ghost projects" ("programas brujas"). He charged that these projects either did not exist, or, if they did, were far from being complete. For example, the feeder roads at Las Pollas and at El Retiro were earmarked at $30,900; yet the ministry said it had completed the project and spent only $4,200. The road at Las Guias was budgeted at $38,400; the ministry spent $5,200 and claimed that the project was completed. Espinosa gave a further example that outraged the assembly: the Mendullo road in the district of La Pintada was in muddy condition; yet the ministry claimed that the road was 100 percent completed at a cost of $50,000.

Although Minister Guerra tried to explain that the discrepancies were due to cost overruns and faulty equipment, the NACR moved to take away the CAM-BID project from the ministry and give the community boards the task of community road building.

On speculation, the public works scandal as uncovered and exposed by Espinosa may have been the result of an administrative change initiated by Torrijos, or the result of the representatives' desire to have the CAM-BID program transferred to the community level, or the result of the combined effect of these two factors. Nevertheless, this scandal and the resulting changes constituted a major setback to the centralizing forces within the administration and was another example of the representatives' struggle to increase their economic participation and relevancy.[28]

The Puerto Obaldia Case. While on the surface this case appeared as a customs house swindle and a government infringement on traditional Indian rights, the details of the situation suggest the traffic of both drugs and contraband goods.

Puerto Obaldia is a port on San Blas, the island group populated by the Cuna Indians, who have a substantial degree of autonomy from the mainland government. However, there were a number of representatives to the NACR from San Blas. In 1973 two of these representatives, Placido Tejada and Sixto Sotomayor, brought charges against a minor customs official working at Puerto Obaldia. The charges were cheating the national treasury, violating maritime law, contraband, and suspicion of **trafficking in drugs.**[29]

Sotomayor explained that ships en route from Colombia or the Colon Free Zone would put into Puerto Obaldia at night without flags, unload, and then take off. Tejada confirmed what Sotomayor said and added that he had verified that the customs officer was also charging higher customs duties to Colombian merchants, who in turn passed on the higher costs to the San Blas merchants. These allegations and implications were rendered more credible in view of the fact that the minister of the treasury, Sanchiz, a friend of the customs official, failed to act on the complaint made by the representatives.

This case had broader ramifications because it could be interpreted as a direct consequence of the increase in government taxes on liquor and luxury items introduced in 1973.[30] The government was unable to control the contraband of such items, particularly in the area of the Colon Free Zone. The Free Zone handled hundreds of millions of dollars' worth of goods each year, officially destined for re-export. However, when ships pulled into Puerto Obaldia en route from the Colon Free Zone without any identifying flags, then it was fair to assume that not only Free Zone goods were smuggled into Panama via Puerto Obaldia. It was also highly likely that drugs from Colombia were being introduced in this manner as well.

Minister Sanchiz, president of the Colon Free Zone Merchants Association, was asked to reply to the charges. He admitted having known the customs officer for twenty years, but denied he had any special relations with him. Immediately following Sanchiz's reply, Cesar Pardo of Cocle moved that the NACR form a special judicial committee to conduct a "grand jury" hearing to consider these and other charges. However, Representative Jaramillo of Cocle intervened in the debate, referring to the Puerto Obaldia case as a rather small matter and requesting that the assembly consider a motion to ask Torrijos to speak. Torrijos entered the hall, spoke on an unrelated matter for one minute, and the meeting was adjourned.[31]

A few months later, Materno Vasquez (populist leader and a principal player in Torrijos's regime) was appointed president of the Supreme Court and supported Sanchiz's claims that the Puerto Obaldia case had been properly investigated by the Ministry of the Treasury and the Ministry of Government and Justice. The customs official was found innocent of all charges.[32]

The NACR was therefore denied the right to exercise its constitutional duty of overseeing the bureaucracy. In this case, an issue that was viewed by the administration as damaging to its image and threatening to its power and authority was glossed over and finally dismissed.

Conclusion

As was the case with the peasant settlements, the community boards were not adequately structured or financed to bring about either extensive rural growth or meaningful local and regional economic development. The boards were primarily political bodies assigned certain economic responsibilities without the skills, financial resources, land and/or labor to perform the tasks set. Moreover, the boards were impeded--politically and bureaucratically--from taking creative steps to obtain the resources to carry out their obligations. Local vested interests and entrenched attitudes compounded the difficulties.

Nevertheless, it was expected that under such conditions the community boards would realize certain specific goals, such as adjusting the rural income imbalance, modernizing rural agricultural production, increasing the number of industrial enterprises located in rural areas, and, in general, stabilizing rural communities. At best, the boards, with the support of state loan guarantees, affected the income level of a few individuals and encouraged some cash crop production and small-scale manufacturing. Otherwise, the boards had to compete with private interests in the development of the rural sector.

On the other hand, the community boards were dependent on the NLC, on MIDA, and on other bureaucracies for such things as feasibility studies and disbursement of funds. They also had to submit to government monitoring or even managing of some projects. The role of the bureaucrat in such activities was justified on technical grounds. But it also served the political function of maintaining the community boards as dependent and ineffective as self-managing enterprises. The success or failure of most projects depended to a great extent on the relations between representatives and their patrons in the regime.

NOTES

1. *Constitucion Politica de la Republica, 1972* (Panama), p. 78.

2. According to Eric De Leon, one of the architects of the San Miguelito project, the concept of a community representative was borrowed from the San Miguelito experiment.

3. The juridical and political status of the three additional members of the community board remained extremely vague, if not confused.

4. The coercive powers of the urban *corregidor* came under attack in 1974: the radical Center for Law Students of the University of Panama introduced a bill to the NLC to reform the urban administrative justice system. Even Torrijos wanted to modify the *corregidors*' powers. But the urban representatives, the district mayors, and the urban municipal police all saw their own power linked to that of the *corregidor* and they opposed any change in the status quo. The proposals for change were dropped.

5. One such case came to light in an interview with a representative from Cocle in August 1974. Unable to obtain the help of a military zone commander of the National Guard, the representative reached Gen. Torrijos, who in turn instructed the local commander to send military vehicles to help the representative with a local building project.

6. Between 1972 and 1974 there were at least three successful actions by the National Assembly to remove three governors.

7. According to Article 134, a representative may lose his/her seat if he/she changes residence, commits a crime, or is recalled by the community.

8. See Eusebio Marchosky, "Asamblea Representativa?" *Dialogo Social*, no. 54 (March 1974).

9. See Republic of Panama, NACR, *Diario de los Debates* 1 (Panama, 1972), pp. 118-20. And in 1974 some representatives were calling for the removal of Altamirano Duque (minister of sports and culture and a member of the bourgeoisie). Carlos Espino (president of the Assembly) opposed the move and reminded the representatives that "we are all happy that the National

Legislative Commission refrains from applying the law governing our recall; this, of course, is because we all agree that the community representative should be protected since we are the pillars of the revolution. In that same spirit we should confront the bureaucrats but not ask for their removal from office." Diario de los Debates 1 (1974), p. 131.

10. Interview with Feliciana Grajales, October 1974.

11. See Diario de los Debates 2 (1974), p. 659.

12. Ibid., p. 668.

13. In effect, the representatives were calling for decentralization of governmental functions and real and effective participation for the municipal bodies and community boards. On the other hand, Torrijos was willing only to transfer some ministries, such as the Ministry of Agricultural Development and the Ministry of Public Works, to the interior.

14. For an insightful discussion on populist structures and fascist ones with respect to their attitude toward opposition structures, see Roger Bartra, "La Mediacion Democratica y la Democracia sin Mediacion," Estudios Sociales Centroamericanos, no. 16 (January-April 1977).

15. Dr. Esquivel was nominated in 1984 to the presidency by the United People's Electoral Front (FREPU). FREPU was composed of leftist and progressive groups and organizations.

16. From more than fifty interviews with representatives and several visits to dozens of communities, we observed this conflict between community boards and health committees. We also found one interesting exception in Chorrillo, where the representative and the head of the health committee cooperated with one another against the corregidor.

17. Diario de los Debates 3 (1974), p. 802.

18. By 1974 Panama had to turn to the more expensive London money market for public as well as private loans. Panama was paying interest rates as high as 12 percent for short-term loans.

19. The issue was fully debated in the 1974 annual meeting of NACR. See Diario de los Debates 2 (1974), pp. 430-36.

20. Interview with Abdiel Perez, representative of the *corregimiento* of Guarare, Los Santos, August 1974.

21. Even in Progreso, Chiriqui, where the most successful peasant settlements were located, the peasants had to look for employment part of the year. In Cocle the representative of El Coco was expectant that the government-sponsored industrial port project at Vacamonte would provide jobs. In any case, the closer to an urban area (especially in Panama and Colon cities), the lesser chance of success for local projects, whether they be sponsored by peasant settlements or community boards. The peasant/worker was at all times hopeful to find a job in an urban area. We owe this insight to Simeon Gonzalez, who at the time was an administrator with the Department of Social Development of the Ministry of Agricultural Development.

22. This was reconstructed by interviews with the representative from Pocri, Aguadulce, and with residents and workers of the Nestle's processing complex, May 1974.

23. Compania Vista Alegre, S.A. had some rather prominent shareholders: a brother of Lt. Col. Noriega; the wife of the president of the Republic (Basilio Lakas); a sister of Gen. Torrijos; and the husband of the representative from San Francisco de las Caletas (Doris Vargas de Rosas). This information was obtained in an interview with the representative of Vista Alegre, October 1974.

24. Interview with the representative of Atalaya, October 1974.

25. Interview with the representative of Parita, October 1974.

26. In 1965 the national government, autonomous and semiautonomous agencies, and municipal agencies had 48,986 employees and by 1975 they had 84,752. These figures were taken from Andres Achong, *La Fuerza de Trabajo en Panama Avances de Investigacion: MOVIMIENTO OBRERO* (Panama, 1979), p. 19.

27. Ministry of Public Works, *Memoria* (Panama, 1974).

28. For complete details of the scandal, see *Diario de los Debates* 2 (1974), pp. 704-7.

29. See *Diario de los Debates* 2 (1973), pp. 498-510.

30. See Robert Looney, *The Economic Development of Panama* (New York, 1976), p. 123.

31. *Diario de los Debates* 2 (1973), p. 512.

32. *Diario de los Debates* 2 (1974), p. 410.

7

Conclusion

Neither caudillos like Anastasio Somoza nor the oligarchies of other Central American countries have been able to meet the political demands for both stability and popular participation without fraud or repression. Neither have they been able and willing to risk their economic preeminence by presiding over economic reforms sought by social groups inside and outside their countries. This resistance to change has brought disequilibrium and stagnation economically and instability and institutionalized violence politically.

The reformist experiment of Omar Torrijos represented a significant exception to this regional rule. There is no question that the general and the National Guard wielded effective power within Panama. On the other hand, an anti-oligarchical, anticolonialist, and strongly nationalist regime allowed the voices of important social groups to be heard for the first time while simultaneously securing relative tranquility.

What were the elements of the Torrijos experiment as of 1975? In light of subsequent developments, what was its significance for the history of Panama's politics?

Elements of the Torrijos Experiment

The Torrijos regime's reformism would not have occurred at all had it not been for the bankruptcy of the oligarchy's rule. (Costa Rica was the only country in Central America where the civilian elite was able to sustain constitutional rule over a long period.) Throughout the twentieth century the Panamanian elite had failed to satisfy the aspirations of the Panamanian people for a better standard of living and the restoration of national sovereignty. Unable to establish its legitimacy in popular eyes, it had faced crises of hegemony in the

1920s, 1940s, and 1960s. Popular movements had arisen on all three occasions to frustrate what was portrayed as appeasement by those in power and to foster widespread instability. Through repression, the oligarchy--or the military on its behalf--had repressed the symptoms of unrest but not the cause.

A telling indication of the oligarchy's inability to become a permanent ruling class was the continuing political prominence of the heretic, Arnulfo Arias Madrid. Three times the oligarchy was unable to field a candidate able to match Arias's appeal, even though it was never in doubt that he was intent on a radical change in the National Guard's role in the political system. Three times Arias had to be removed from power, making a mockery of the traditional rules of political competition.

The second element of Torrijos's reformism was the relative distance from politics the National Guard had maintained before 1968. As a result, it existed as an alternate power center, unbound by past commitments of either a social or ideological sort. The Guard had not been more or less permanently in power as the self-proclaimed guardian against the communist threat, as the military had in Guatemala. It had never <u>become</u> the oligarchy as a result of the unlimited power of a strongman, as was the case in Nicaragua (although General Remon might have become a Somoza had he not been assassinated). It was never co-opted by the civilian elite, as the Salvadoran armed forces had been by the fourteen families. More like the Honduran military, the Panamanian National Guard was relatively independent of the civilian elite and intervened in politics when that was the only way to restore a measure of political stability.

Third, the Guard itself was divided over what to do once it seized power in 1968. The faction under Colonel Martinez wished to impose military rule, a la Nicaragua or Guatemala. Colonels Silvera and Sanjur wished to stick to tradition and return power to the oligarchy after allowing the dust to settle. Torrijos led a faction that grasped the possibility of an alternative.

Torrijos would not have had the opportunity to try to realize his vision had he not been a superb political tactician. He bided his time in the wake of the coup, waiting for his rivals to make their bid for preeminence. Martinez moved in February 1969, and was quickly dispatched to Miami. Silvera and Sanjur tried in November of that same year while Torrijos was out of the country, but his loyal allies facilitated his return in time to foil the plot.

The fourth factor contributing to Torrijos's success was the existence of the canal issue itself. The American presence fueled nationalistic passions that no political leader could ignore and few could control. Yet a populist leader who could rein in the radicalism inspired by the canal was in a position to use the threat of popular movements to increase his power vis-a-vis the oligarchy and the United States.

The fifth and central element of the Torrijos regime was its approach to politics. For Panama and Central America it was a "new politics" in which the military would demonstrate itself more effective than the oligarchy in meeting the demands for expanded participation and achieving national imperatives, yet all the while preserving essential stability.

It was therefore necessary to restructure the channels of participation in such a way that the popular classes could be directly involved in politics for the first time and, as a result, would provide support for the government when it challenged the oligarchy or the United States. Torrijos moved quickly to forge an alliance between the military and the communist Party of the People, which was the organization most capable of mobilizing the mass movement. In a related move, the regime drafted a labor code that gave many new rights and privileges to urban workers.

Early on, Torrijos also saw the need to create institutional links with the marginal segments of Panamanian society--the urban squatters of San Miguelito and the landless in the countryside. Already organized by the Church, San Miguelito could be a source of political volatility if not co-opted for the ends of the regime. That was accomplished by the third anniversary of the October Revolution. In the rural areas, the system of peasant settlements had a dual purpose. Economically, it was hoped that these collectives would generate new jobs and agricultural production for markets both home and abroad. Politically, the settlements became a new support group for the regime, strengthened its alliance with the Party of the People (since the communists were given control over the National Confederation of Peasant Settlements), and in the process co-opted the long-time leaders of the peasant movement.

In pursuing these initiatives, the regime was careful not to alienate the oligarchy. Nonconfrontation and class cooperation were the watchwords, even in the face of resentment on the part of the groups concerned. This nonprovocative approach became even more pronounced during the economic crisis of 1973 and 1974, when the regime shifted its economic strategy in an effort to encourage the loyalty of the oligarchy as the challenge to the United States became even more complicated. As a result, the peasant settlements were judged more on an economic than political basis.

In 1972, by which time these experiments were already under way, Torrijos turned to establishing a constitutional system that would institutionalize the access of the popular classes to politics. The result was a system of elected representatives who were to have a role in government at each level of the hierarchy, along with appointed officials.

Yet the regime did not wish to pay for the resulting enhancement of its legitimacy with a grant of power to the new actors in the system. In the constitutional debates on the role of the representatives and the powers of the National Assembly of Community Representatives, the drafters of the new charter fought back every effort to give the elected delegates a seat at the decision-making table. They were useful as a national sounding board, but as little else.

The exception to this rule was at the lowest level, that of the community boards. There the representative was expected to be the catalyst for small-scale economic development projects and Torrijos's eyes and ears concerning the performance of local bureaucrats. In this regard, however, the representatives often lacked the financial resources to support the projects designed, or the political clout to remove the obstacles placed in their way by vested interests.

The Fate of the Torrijismo

The true test of the Torrijos reforms is how well the resulting political system fares in the crises--economic, foreign policy, political succession, etc.--that inevitably beset it. Only if Torrijismo is capable of either preventing or surviving new crises of hegemony will it be judged a significant improvement over its predecessors. Although an assessment of post-1975 is a subject worthy of a full-length study, even a cursory review of recent developments is suggestive.

In 1977 the Torrijos regime concluded a canal treaty with the United States that did not come up to nationalistic aspirations. Panama obtained greater economic control over the canal and greater sovereignty over the zone. On the other hand, the Carter-Torrijos treaty legalized the controversial U.S. military bases and preserved Washington's administration of the canal and its right to intervene to defend the canal. For the moment, the United States and Panama are trying to keep the implementation of the canal treaty from becoming a political issue. But it remains an explosive one, especially for the black workers in the canal area, and the military will not be immune from the accusations of any future nationalistic mass movement.

Second, the economy never fully recovered from the crisis of the mid-seventies. If anything it worsened, the worst since the Great Depression. As a result of the worldwide recession, Panama had accumulated an external debt of $3.5 billion as of early 1985. Unemployment was in the range of 20 percent, with no strategy for putting people back to work. Indeed, if the government of Panama chooses to follow the International Monetary Fund road of austerity out of its balance of payments problems, it risks social instability and disorder.

Third, the economic crisis has accelerated the recomposition of the coalition supporting the regime. The new approach taken toward the peasant settlements in late 1974 was confirmed, and the national confederation was defunded, preventing it from continuing its efforts among the peasantry. The antilabor tendencies that were apparent in 1975 strengthened as time went on. In December 1976 Law 95 was passed, amending the labor code to take back from workers and salaried employees the gains they had received from the original 1972 code, particularly in the areas of collective bargaining and job stability.

As a result, the trade unions and professional organizations began to turn against the regime, pressing for the repeal of Law 95. For the first time in Panamanian history, the labor movement assumed leadership of the popular movement. In 1979 the teachers union struck for several weeks, creating a political crisis for the presidency of Aristides Royo. (After Royo denounced the teachers as unpatriotic, the oligarchy went so far as to offer political and material support to the strikers.) In March 1980 the National Council of Organized Workers (COWATO) called a forty-eight-hour general strike.

Partly as a result of the economic crisis, and partly under pressure from the Carter administration, Torrijos decided on a return to civilian rule. As he moved toward the center of the Panamaniam political spectrum, he took steps to restructure the political process to allow greater participation by the oligarchy, modifying the political articles of the 1972 constitution to allow the revival of the traditional parties. Local elections were set for 1980 and direct presidential and legislative elections for 1984.

The right wing organized the National Opposition Union (UNO). Included were the Panamenista party led by Arnulfo Arias, the Christian Democrats, and the lesser right-wing groups. Torrijos responded by organizing the Democratic Revolutionary party (PRD). It incorporated elements of the middle strata, remnants of peasants and workers groups, and, most importantly, elements of the bourgeoisie linked to international capital. At the same time, Torrijos purged the most class-conscious and radical cadres of the original revolution, affecting even individuals occupying ministerial and subministerial positions. Ideologically the PRD was linked to the Socialist International, but it lacked a coherent ideology and relied on Torrijos to strike a balance between the left and right wing of the party.

Then on July 31, 1981, that unifying element was removed, as Torrijos was killed in a mysterious plane crash in Cocle province. The National Guard (renamed the National Defense Forces [NDF] in 1984) was racked by high-level power struggles as it sought to preserve its dominance. Eventually Antonio Manuel Noriega emerged as first among equals.

Compounding Panama's problems was the fact that the period between Torrijos's death and the presidential elections in May 1984 was one of increased tensions within the Central American region. The Reagan administration chose to pursue a military solution to the problems of poverty, hunger, and inequality in the region. The United States was not happy about Panama's participation in the Contadora process, which sought a negotiated solution to the conflict in Central America. The U. S. Southern Command, headed by General Paul Gorman, pressured the NDF to participate in joint exercises with the American military designed to intimidate Nicaragua. After Gen. Noriega initially agreed, the government reversed itself.

The elections of May 1984 pitted Dr. Nicholas Ardito Barletta, former minister of economic policy and planning and then vice president of the World Bank, against the old nemesis of the Guard, Arnulfo Arias. Barletta was backed by the military and the most important sections of the bourgeoisie and international finance. His electoral coalition included the PRD and the Liberal and Republican parties. Arias headed the UNO coalition, composed of the Authentic Panamenista party, the Christian Democrats, and others. The popular groups alienated from the regime were wooed by the Independent Revolutionary Workers' party, which together with other progressive forces organized the United People's Electoral Front and backed the candidacy of Dr. Renan Esquivel. (The Left's principal accomplishment was getting over 30,000 signatures to register for the election).

In his campaign, Barletta--and the military commanders who spoke in his favor--emphasized the preservation of Panama's vaunted social peace. He spoke very little of the economic crisis, except to express a preference for private capital and export promotion. It was no surprise that Barletta failed to arouse impassioned support, especially among the popular classes. Arias, on the other hand, as a result of mass discontent with the regime, retained broad popularity.

After two weeks of vote counting and amid accusations of widespread fraud, Barletta was declared the winner by a margin of less than one-half of 1 percent. The military's effort to legitimize its rule had failed.

Acronyms

BDA: Banco Desarrollo Agropecuario
[Agricultural Development Bank]

BID: Banco Inter-americano de Desarrollo
[Inter-American Development Bank]

CIAP: Comite Inter-Americano para la Alvarza del Progress
[Committee for Inter-American Alliance]

CNL: Consejo Nacional de Legislacion
[National Legislative Council]

CNT: Confederacion Nacional de Trabajadores
[National Workers Confederation]

CONAC: Confederacion Nacional de Asentamientos Campesinos
[National Confederation of Peasant Settlements]

CONEP: Consejo Nacional de Empresas Privados
[National Confederation of Private Enterprise]

CRA: Comision de Reforma Agraria
[Agrarian Reform Commission]

DIGEDECOM: Direccion General para el Desarrollo de la Comunidad
[General Directorate for Community Development]

DINRA: Direccion Nacional de Reforma Agraria
[National Department for Agrarian Reform]

FEP: Federacion de Estudiantes Panamenos
[Federation of Panamanian Students]

IFARHU: Instituto de Formacion y Adiestramiento de Recurses Humanos
[Institute of Training and Human Resources]

IFE:	Instituto de Fomento Economico [Institute of Economic Promotion]
IICA:	Instituto Interamericano de Ciencias Agricolas [Interamerican Institute of Agricultural Sciences]
INAC:	Instituto Nacional de Cultural [National Institute of Culture]
INCAE:	Instituto Centroamericano de Administracion de Empresas [Central American Institute of Business Administration]
IVU:	Instituto de Vivienda y Urbanizacion [Housing and Urbanization Institute]
MIDA:	Ministerio de Desarrollo Agropecuario [Ministry of Agricultural Development]
MUNDO:	Movimiento de Unificacion Nacional, Desarrollo y Orientacion [Movement of National Unification, Development and Guidance]
NACR:	Assamblea Nacional de Representantes de Corregimientos [National Assembly of Community Representatives]
NDF:	Fuezas de Defensa Nacional [National Defense Forces]
NLC:	Comision Nacional de Legislacion [National Legislative Commission]
PRD:	Partido Revolucionario Democratico [Democratic Revolutionary Party]
UNO:	Union Nacional de Oposicion [National Opposition Union]

Appendixes

APPENDIX 1

DISTRIBUTION OF WORK FORCE
REPUBLIC OF PANAMA

SECTOR	1960	1965	1970	1974	1975
Private Businesses	40,880 (44.9%)	58,142 (49.3%)	86,439 (50.22%)	119,693 (52.82%)	117,344 (50.95%)
Banana Growing Zones	10,255 (11.3%)	10,994 (9.2%)	15,738 (9.14%)	10,168 (4.48%)	11,176 (4.85%)
National Government	23,884 (26.2%)	27,359 (23.2%)	41,380 (24.04%)	53,317 (23.52%)	54,823 (23.80%)
Institutions (Autonomous and Semiautonomous)	4,973 (5.5%)	8,852 (7.5%)	11,883 (6.9%)	25,704 (11.34%)	29,929 (12.99%)
Municipalities			2,295 (1.33%)	3,139 (1.38%)	2,562 (1.11%)
Canal Zone	11,033 (12.1%)	12,775 (10.8%)	14,367 (8.34%)	14,635 (6.45%)	14,447 (6.27%)
TOTAL	91,002 (100%)	118,032 (100%)	172,100 (100%)	226,602 (100%)	230,281 (100%)

Source: Series _Estadistica de Trabajo_, D.E.C.

APPENDIX 2

GROWTH INDEX OF THE WORK FORCE (1960–1975)

REPUBLIC OF PANAMA

SECTOR	1960	1965	1970	1974	1975
Private Businesses	100.0	142.2	211.4	192.7	287.8
Banana Growing Zones	100.0	106.3	153.5	99.2	109.0
National Government	100.0	114.5	173.3	223.2	229.5
Institutions (Autonomous and Semiautonomous)	100.0	178.0	238.9	519.9	601.8
Municipalities	100.0		141.1	193.0	219.1
Canal Zone	100.0	115.8	130.3	132.7	131.0
TOTAL WORK FORCE	100.0	129.7	189.1	248.9	254.1

Source: Series *Estadistica de Trabajo*, D.E.C.

APPENDIX 3

NUMBER OF PEASANT SETTLEMENTS AND FAMILIES ORGANIZED PER PROVINCE (1969–1972)

REPUBLIC OF PANAMA

	1969*		1970*		1971**		1972***		TOTALS	
PROVINCE	NO. SETTLEMENTS	ORGANIZED FAMILIES	NO. SETTLEMENTS	ORGANIZED FAMILIES	NO. SETTLEMENTS	ORGANIZED FAMILIES	NO. SETTLEMENTS	ORGANIZED FAMILIES	NO. SETTLEMENTS	ORGANIZED FAMILIES
Cocle	6	270	1	26	7	207	1	43	15	546
Colon	4	182	3	165	6	209	2	77	15	633
Chiriqui	2	99	8	553	8	355	2	68	20	1,075
Herrera	4	130	–	–	5	168	2	27	11	325
Los Santos	1	30	2	43	2	49	–	–	5	122
Panama	6	298	6	408	9	418	5	114	26	1,238
Veraguas	10	290	4	268	13	498	10	328	37	1,384
TOTAL	33	1,299	24	1,463	50	1,904	22	657	129	5,323

Sources: *Comision de Reforma Agraria, Memoria 1971 (Panama, 1971), p. 7.

**Comision de Reforma Agraria, Direccion de Desarrollo Campesino 1973, I Semestre (Panama, 1973), p. 3.

***Comision de Reforma Agraria, Informe Estadistico, I Semestre 1972 (Panama, 1972), p. 2.

APPENDIX 4

GOVERNMENT CREDIT TO PEASANT SETTLEMENTS (1970–1972)

REPUBLIC OF PANAMA

PROVINCE	1970*			1971*			1972**		
	NO. SETTLEMENTS	CREDIT IN MILLION	PERCENT OF CREDIT	NO. SETTLEMENTS	CREDIT IN MILLION	PERCENT OF CREDIT	NO. SETTLEMENTS	CREDIT IN MILLION	PERCENT OF CREDIT
Chiriqui	12	31.6	41.0	15	150.5	58.0	23	117.1	54.9
Veraguas	15	14.9	19.5	15	35.9	14.0	28	27.3	12.8
Cocle	7	10.1	13.0	11	26.7	10.0	15	29.1	13.7
Panama	12	8.1	11.0	13	19.3	7.0	18	23.3	10.9
Colon	8	5.8	7.5	8	13.3	5.0	13	9.5	4.5
Herrera	4	3.7	5.0	7	8.8	3.5	7	6.1	2.9
Los Santos	3	2.3	3.0	4	5.1	2.5	4	0.7	0.3
TOTAL	61	76.5	100.0	73	259.6	100.0	108	213.1	100.0

Sources: *Comision de Reforma Agraria, Compendio Estadistico 163 de 1971 (Panama, 1972), pp. 44-51.

**Comision de Reforma Agraria, Informe Estadistico II Semestre, Direccion de Programacion (Panama, 1972), pp. 24-27.

APPENDIX 5

COUNCIL OF STATE
BY NAME, OFFICE, PROFESSION, AND
COUNTRY OF STUDY
(1977)

REPUBLIC OF PANAMA

NAME	OFFICE	PROFESSION	PLACE STUDIED
Demetrio B. Lakas	President	Civil Engineer	United States
Gerardo Gonzalez	Vice President	Economist	Panama and Chile
Ricardo Rodriguez	Interior	Attorney	Panama
Juan Antonia Tack	Foreign Affairs	Historian	Panama and Paris
N. Ardito Barletta	Economics	Economist	United States
Miguel Sanchiz	Treasury	Civil Service	N/A
Fernando Manfredo	Commerce and Industry	Business Administration	N/A
Rolando Murgas	Labor	Attorney	Panama and Rome
Abraham Saied	Health	Doctor	Panama and U.S.
Jose de la Ossa	Housing	Financier	N/A
Tomas Guerra	Public Works	Civil Engineer	N/A
Aristides Royo	Education	Attorney	Madrid
Ruben D. Paredes	Agricultural Development	Military	Nicaragua

Source: Renato Pereira, Panama: Fuerzas Armadas y Politica (Panama, 1979), p. 142.

APPENDIX 6

NATIONAL LEGISLATIVE COMMISSION MEMBERS BY NAME, PROFESSION, AND COUNTRY OF STUDY (1977)

REPUBLIC OF PANAMA

NAME	PROFESSION	PLACE STUDIED
Adolfo Ahumada	Attorney	Panama
Marcelino Jaen	Attorney	Panama
Eligio Salas	Attorney	Panama
Nilson Espino	Agricultural Engineer	Panama
Balbino Moreno	Administrator	Panama and U.S.
Ruben D. Herrera	Economist Ph.D.	Panama and Mexico
E.P. Valladares	Financier	U.S.
Carlos P. Herrera	Former Priest	Rome

Source: Renato Pereira, *Panama: Fuerzas Armadas y Politica* (Panama, 1979), p. 143.

APPENDIX 7

JOINT CHIEFS OF STAFF BY RANK, NAME, DIVISION, AND TRAINING PROFILE (1975)

REPUBLIC OF PANAMA

RANK	NAME	ACADEMY	YEAR	DIVISION	OFFICE
Brigadier General	Omar Torrijos H.	El Salvador	1952	Infantry	Chief of Staff
Colonel	Rodrigo Garcia	El Salvador	1955	Infantry	Assistant Chief
Lieutenant Colonel	Florencio Flores	Nicaragua	1955	Infantry	G-1, of P.C.
" "	Ruben D. Paredes	Nicaragua	1957	Infantry	G-1, Personnel
" "	Manuel Noriega	Peru	1962	Engineer Corps	G-2, Intelligence
" "	Armando Contreras	Nicaragua	1958	Infantry	G-3, Operations
" "	Armando Bellido	Rank, Panama	....	Admin.	G-4, Admin.
" "	Gaspar A. Suarez	El Salvador	1950	Infantry	G-5, Civic Action
" "	Manuel A. Arauz	Nicaragua	1957	Infantry	Transit Auth.
Major	Roberto Diaz H.	Peru	1961	Civil Guard	Exec. Secty.

*Source: Renato Pereira, Panama: Fuerzas Armadas y Politica (Panama, 1979), p. 146.

Selected Bibliography

Accion Comunal. Newspaper of Communal Action.

Acuna, Alfredo V. Aspectos de la Reforma Agraria Panamena. Panama: Direccion Nacional de Reforma Agraria, Ministerio de Desarrollo Agropecuario, 1973.

Adames, Carlos. "Salvamento de Voto en el Recurso de Amparo contra el Presidente de la Republica, Sr. Marco A. Robles (1968)." Tareas, no. 27, pp. 83-96.

Aguilar, Alonso. Pan-Americanism from Monroe to the Present. New York: Monthly Review Press, 1968.

Aguilera, Rodolfo, Jr. 50 Millas de Heroicidad (Realto Sobre el Canal). 6th ed. Panama: Impresora Panama, 1961.

Alba, C., Manuel Maria. Cronologia de los Gobernantes de Panama, 1510-1932. Panama: Imprenta Nacional, 1935.

Alberti, G. "The Breakdown of Provincial Urban Power Structure and the Rise of Peasant Movements." Sociologia Ruralis 12 (1972):315-33.

Alfaro, Ricardo J. Limites entre Panama y Costa Rica. Panama, 1913.

________. "Medio Siglo de Relaciones entre Panama y los Estados Unidos." In Panama y los Estados Unidos ante el Problema del Canal. Panama: Faculty of Law and Political Science, University of Panama, 1966.

Almengor, Luis A., et al. Sintesis (Historica del Barrio del Chorrillo). Panama: Edicion de la Junta Communal del Chorrillo, 1974.

Alvarez Icaza M., Jose. "Indignacion Popular en Panama: La Iglesia y el Regimen Militar al Borde de la Ruptura." 1971. Circulated by L.A.P. Service, Washington, D.C.

Anderson, Charles W. _Politics and Economic Change in Latin America_. Princeton, N.J.: Van Nostrand Co., 1967.

Araica, Hildebrando A. "Notas Sobre el Crecimiento Demografico y la Urbanizacion de Panama." _International Union for Scientific Study of Population_. Sydney, 1967, pp. 722-28.

Asentamientos Campesinos y la Reforma Agraria. Select newspaper clippings (1969-1973) from local newspapers in Panama's National Library.

Bambirra, Vania. _El Capitalismo Dependiente Latinoamericano_. 3rd ed. Mexico: Siglo XXI, 1976.

Banco de Desarrollo Agropecuario. _Memoria_. 1974.

Barrios Gomez, Francisco, President of National Executive Committee of National Association of Peasants, Colombia. Letter of the Association to Mons. Marcos McGrath, Archbishop of Panama, n.d.

Bartra, Roger. "La Mediacion Democratica y Democracia Sin Mediacion." _Estudios Sociales Centroamericanos_, no. 16 (January-April 1977).

Baxter, Richard R., and Carrol, Doris. _The Panama Canal: Background Papers and Proceedings of the 6th Hammarskjold Forum_. New York: Oceana Publications, 1965.

Bayano. Newspaper published in Brooklyn, N.Y., 1973.

Behrendt, Richard. _Problemas y Orientaciones Socio-Economicos para la Post Guerra_. Panama: Instituto de Investigaciones Sociales y Economicas, 1945.

Beleno, Joaquin. _Curundu_. Panama, 1961.

Bemis, Samuel. _Latin American Policy of the United States_. New York: W. W. Norton & Co., 1943.

Benedetti, Adolfo Alberto. _Arnulfo Arias: El Caudillo_. Panama: Editora Humanidad, S.A., 1963.

Bermudez, Julio. "Participacion del Campesino en la Lucha por la Liberacion Nacional." Speech delivered at Panama University's Seminario de Relaciones entre Panama y los Estados Unidos, February 19, 1974.

Bermudez, Ricardo. "Notas Sobre la Crisis de Confianza." Dialogo Social, no. 54 (March 1974).

Bernal, Miguel Antonio. Los Tratados Carter-Torrijos: Una Traicion Historica. Mexico, 1977.

"Bias Bill Becomes Law, Heurtematte's Bill Against Racial Bias OK'd by Solons." The Nation 10, no. 32.

Bock, Philip. Peasants in the Modern World. Albuquerque: University of New Mexico, 1969.

Bolanos, Felix E. "Las Luchas Reinvindicatorias Panamenas." Relaciones Entre Panama y Los Estados Unidos. Panama: Biblioteca Nuevo Panama, 1974, pp. 221-32.

Boletin Informativo. Newspaper of INDESA.

Bravo, Francisco. The Parish of San Miguelito in Panama: History and Pastoral Theological Evaluation. Cuernavaca, Mexico: Centro Intercultural de Documentacion, 1966.

Bryce-Laporte, Roy Simon. "Varias Ideas Sobre el Significado de la Experiencia del Grupo de Origen Afro-antillano de Panama para los Estudios Afro-americanos." Paper delivered at the Fourth National Symposium of Anthropology, Archeology and Ethnohistory, University of Panama, October 1973.

Bullard, Arthur. Panama: The Canal, the Country and the People. New York: Macmillan Company, 1911.

Burgós, Antonio. Panama y su Inmigracion. Panama: Imprenta Nacional, 1913.

Caballero, Jose Maria. "Sobre el Caracter de la Reforma Agraria Peruana." Latin American Perspectives 4 (Summer 1977):145-59.

Cambios. Newspaper published by Guaykucho-NIR in Panama.

Candanedo, Cesar A. La Otra Frontera. Panama, 1962.

Cardoso, F. H., and Weffort, F., eds. America Latina: Ensayos de Interpretacion Sociologico-Politica. 2nd ed. Santiago: Editorial Universitaria, S.A., 1966.

Carles, Ruben D. Victoriano Lorenzo: El Guerrillero de la Tierra de Los Cholos. 2nd ed. Panama: Editorial Litografica, S.A., 1966.

________. Constitucion de Panama Articulo 29. Caracas, 1976.

Carranza, Mario Esteban. Fuerzas Armadas y Estado de Excepcion en America Latina. Mexico: Siglo XXI, 1978.

Castillero Calvo, Alfredo. "Transitismo y Dependencia: El Caso de Panama." Estudios Sociales Centroamericanos, no. 5 (May-August 1973).

________. "Balance y Liquidacion de la Dominacion Espanola." Relaciones entre Panama y los Estados Unidos. Vol. 3. Panama: Biblioteca Nuevo Panama, 1974.

________. "El Oro de California en al Vida Panemena." Relaciones entre Panama y los Estados Unidos. Vol. 3. Panama: Biblioteca Nuevo Panama, 1974.

Castillo, R., Ernesto J. Chiriqui: Ensayo de Monografia de la Provincia de Chiriqui. Panama: Impresora Panama, 1968.

Castro Herrera, Guillermo. Panama 1977. Panama: Centro de Estudios Latinoamericanos "Justo Arosemena," CELA, 1978.

Chavez, A. Lezcano. La Revolucion del Pueblo Panameno y su Filosofia. Panama: Ediciones Panama, 1971.

Christian Science Monitor.

Cinco Ensayos. Panama, n.d.

Claire, Emilio F. "Desigualdad Economica en Panama." Universidad (Organo de la Universidad de Panama), no. 42. Panama:Editorial Universitaria, 1972, pp. 181-205.

Colegio de Ingenieros Agronomos de Panama-CINAP. El Problema del Alto Costo de la Vida en Panama. Panama, 1973.

Collection of Special Editions of Panama's Newspapers 1928-1953 Devoted to the History of Panama and Panama Canal Zone. New York Public Library at 42nd Street.

Confederacion Interamericana de Ganaderos. Proceedings of VIII General Assembly, November 14-18, 1972.

Conferencia Episcopal Panamena. "Comunicado." Document signed by Archbishop Marcos McGrath and several Panamanian bishops, June 14, 1971.

Conte Porras, J. La Rebelion de la Esfinges (Historia del Movimiento Estudiantil Panameno). Panama: Litho-Impresora Panama, S.A., 1978.

Cooley, John Andrew. "The United States and the Panama Canal, 1938-1947: Policy Formulation and Implementation from Munich through the Early Years of the Cold War." Ph.D. dissertation, Ohio State University, 1972.

Correo Popular. An irregular weekly that appeared in 1977 in Panama.

Critica. Newspaper.

Cuevas, Alexander. El Movimiento Inquilinario de 1925. Panama: Ediciones de la Revista Tareas, 1975.

De Jurado, Selma Noriega. Verdad y Miseria de Nuestros Partidos Politicos. Panama: Editora Renovacion, 1978.

De la Cruz, Herrera, Jose. Panama, sus Problemas y sus Hombres--Accion Communal. Panama, n.d.

De la Guardia, Ernesto, Jr. Teoria y Practica de la Democracia (Conversaciones con el Pueblo). Panama, 1960.

De la Guardia, Juan R. Porras. El Multiparticismo de Panama. Bogota: Universidad Javeriana Facultad de Ciencias Juridicas, 1960.

De la Rosa, Albino Ruben. El Nacimiento de una Republica Nueva. Panama: Imprenta Nacional, 1970.

De la Rosa, Diogenes. Ensayos Varios. Panama, n.d.

Del Cid Molina, Miguel Angel, et al. "Estrategia, Plan de Desarrollo Nacional y Politica Economica." Tareas, no. 43 (September 1978).

De Leon, Cesar A. "Significado Historico de la Actual Crisis entre Panama y los Estados Unidos." Speech delivered at "Casa del Periodista," sponsored by Scientific-Cultural Association of Panama, February 26, 1964.

De Leon, Eric. Programa de Desarrollo de la Comunidad del Movimiento de Unificacion Nacional, Desarrollo y Orientacion (MUNDO), Anexo B. Panama, December 1968.

________. "Perspectiva de la Democracia en Panama." September 23, 1970.

________ "Informe Sobre Posesion de las Tierras en San Miguelito." 1971.

Denton, Charles. "Interest Groups in Panama and the Central American Common Market." Inter-American Economic Affairs 21 (1967).

De Roux, Raul. Un Capitulo de Historia Patria o Arnulfo Arias: El Patriota. Panama, 1945.

De Souza, Herbet. Notes on the Socio-Political Situation in Panama. Toronto: Brazilian Studies, 1975.

Di Tella, Torcuato. "Populism and Reform in Latin America." In Obstacles to Change in Latin America, edited by Claudio Veliz. London: Oxford University Press, 1969, pp. 47-74.

Draper, Hal. Karl Marx's Theory of Revolution: State and Bureaucracy. 2 vols. New York: Monthly Review Press, 1977.

Eastin, Nelson. "The Development of Economic Policy in the Republic of Panama." Ph.D. Dissertation, University of Texas at Austin, 1945.

Epocas. Newspaper.

Escobar, Felipe J. El Legado de los Proceres: Ensayo Historico-Politico Sobre la Nacionalidad Panamena. Panama: Imprenta Nacional, 1928.

Escobar, Juan Felipe. Arnulfo Arias o el Credo del Panamenismo 1930-1940. Panama, n.d.

Fabrega F., Ramon. Constituciones de la Republica de Panama (1904-1941-1946). Panama: Agencia Internacional de Publicaciones, S.A., 1969.

Fallas, Carlos Luis. Mamita Yunai. San Jose, Costa Rica: Libreria Lehman, 1978.

Feder, Ernest. The Rape of the Peasantry: Latin America's Landholding System. New York: Anchor Books, 1971.

Fonseca Mora, Ramon. "Movilizacion de los Estudiantes de Leyes." Dialogo Social, no. 57 (June 9, 1974), pp. 36-37.

Fortune, Armando. "Origenes Extra-Africanos y Mestizaje Etnico del Negro Panameno a Comienzos del Siglo XVII." La Epoca 5 (1960):1113-28.

Franco, Munoz, Hernando. Movimiento Obrero Panameno 1914-1921. Panama, n.d.

Frobel, Heinrichs, Kreye. "Export-Oriented Industrialization of Underdeveloped Countries." Monthly Review, November 1978, pp. 22-26.

Galindo, Mario. "Los Partidos Politicos." Dialogo Social, no. 54 (March 1974).

Gallegos, Hector. "Desafio a Los Cristianos." Dialogo Social, no. 46 (June 9, 1973).

Gandasegui, Marco A. La Concentracion del Poder Economico en Panama. Panama, 1967.

________. "La Estructura Agraria en el Desarrollo Nacional." Tareas, no. 24 (April-October 1972), pp. 5-22.

________. "Industrializacion e Inversiones Extranjeras en Panama." Estudios Sociales Centroamericanos 3 (January-April 1974):1-34.

________. "La Lucha de Clases y la Zona del Canal." Cuaderno de Sociologia No. 1. Panama: Asociacion Panamena de Sociologia, 1975.

________. "Cambio Social en el Agro." Documento del II Congreso de Sociologia. Panama: Asociacion Panamena de Sociologia, March 1976.

________. "Liberacion Nacional y los Nuevos Ordenes Sociales." Tareas, no. 40 (October-December 1977).

________, and Gorostiaga, Xabier. Panama, Solo un Canal? Prepared for a permanent seminar on Latin America. Joint project of CELA "Justo Arosemena" and the Center for Social Studies and Action. Mexico, 1978.

________. El Campesinado Panameno. Panama: CELA, 1980.

Garay, Narciso. Panama y las Guerras de los Estados Unidos. Panama, 1930.

Garcia, Antonio. Sociologia de la Reforma Agraria en America Latina. Buenos Aires: Amorrotu Editores, 1973.

Garcia Marguez, Gabriel. "Torrijos: Cruce de Mula y Tigre." Alternative, no. 126 (1977), pp. 2-5.

Georgetown University. Center for Strategic Studies. Panama Canal Issues and Treaty Talks. Special Report, Series #3. Washington, D.C., March 1967.

Goldrich, Daniel. Radical Nationalism: The Political Orientations of Panamanian Law Students. Michigan State University, 1962.

________. Sons of the Establishment. New York: Rand McNally, 1966.

Gonzalez, Epifanio. "Una Injusticia Vivida." Dialogo Social, no. 56 (May 9, 1974), pp. 34-36.

Gonzalez H., Simeon. Panama: Dependencia Economica y Desarrollo Politico (Un Analisis de los "Estratos Medios"). Panama: Ediciones de la Libreria Internacional Ltd., 1974.

________. Industrializacion y Reproduccion Capitalista en Panama. Panama: Centro de Estudios Latinoamericanos "Justo Arosemena," 1977.

Gorostiaga, Xabier. "La Inversion Extranjera en Panama." La Inversion Extranjera en Centroamerica. EDUCA, 1974.

________. Los Banqueros del Imperio: Los Centros Financieros Internacionales en los Paises Sub-desarrollados. Costa Rica: Editorial Universitaria Centroamericana, 1978.

Goytia, Victor Florencio. Biografia de una Republica. Panama, 1953.

Grannum de Lewis, Catalina N. Los Trabajadores Panamenos de Ascendencia Antillana en la Zona del

Canal de Panama. Panama: Centro de Estudios Latinoamericanos "Justo Arosemena," 1979.

Graziani, Giovanni. American Latina, Imperialismo y Subdesarrollo. Mexico: Editorial Diogenes, S.A., 1971.

Griffin, Keith. Under-Development in Spanish America. London: George Allen and Unwin Ltd., 1969.

Guaykucho-NIR (PRT). Las Capas Medias y el Proceso de las Relaciones entre Panama y los Estados Unidos. Panama, n.d.

Guizado, Jose Ramon. El Extrano Asesinato del Presidente Ramon. Barcelona: Editorial Linomonograph, 1964.

Gutierrez, Samuel A. Marginalidad y Vivienda: El Problema de las "Barriadas Brujas" en al Ciudad de Panama. Panama: Talleras de Editoral Litografica, S.A., 1974.

Harries-Jenkins, Gwyn, and Van Doorn, Jacques, eds. The Military and the Problem of Legitimacy. London Sage Studies in International Sociology 2. London, 1972.

Haskins, Frederic J. The Panama Canal. Garden City, N.J.: Doubleday, Page & Co., 1913.

Heckandon, Stanley. Los Asentamientos Campesinos: Una Experiencia Panamena en Reforma Agraria. Panama: Ministerio de Planificacion y Politica Economica, 1973.

Herrera, Francisco. "La Zona Indigena del Distrito de Las Palmas, Veraguas, y el Proceso de la Politizacion." Hombre y Cultura 2 (December 1970).

Herrera P., Ruben D. La Necesidad de Cambios Sociales en el Desarrollo Economico de Panama. Panama, 1974.

________. La Empresa Estatal en Panama. Panama: Comision de Legislacion No. 6, 1977.

Herrero, Federico. Guia para la Elaboracion de un Programa de Reforma Agraria. Vol. 1. Guatemala: Instituto Interamericano de Ciencias Agricolas, Organizacion de Estados Americanos, 1973.

"Historia de la Compania Panamena de Fuerza y Luz." *Revista Loteria*, no. 200 (July 1972).

Hodges, Donald C. *The Latin American Revolution: Politics and Strategy from Apro-Marxism to Guevarism*. New York: William Morrow & Co., 1974.

Horowitz, Irving Louis, ed. *Masses in Latin America*. New York: Oxford University Press, 1970.

________, et al. *Latin American Radicalism; A Documentary Report on Left and Nationalist Movements*. New York: Vintage Books, 1969.

Hudson, Michael. *Super Imperialism: The Economic Strategy of American Empire*. New York: Holt, Rhinehart and Winston, 1972.

Huizer, Gerrit. *El Potencial Revolucionario del Campesino en America Latina*. Mexico: Siglo XXI, 1973.

Huntington, Samuel P. *Political Order in Changing Societies*. New Haven: Yale University Press, 1968.

Ianni, Octavio. *La Formacion del Estado Populista en America Latina*. Mexico: Serie Popular Era, 1975.

Ickis, John. *San Miguelito: Case Studies No. 1, 2, 3 and 4*. Instituto Centroamericano de Administracion de Empresas (INCAE), 1972.

Instituto Interamericano de Ciencias Agricolas (IICA). IV Interamerican Meeting of Agrarian Reform Executives. Panama, May 14-20, 1972.

International Labor Office. *Informe al Gobierno de Panama Sobre Salario Minimo*. 1964.

Jaen Suarez, Omar. *Las Estructuras Agrarias en las Sabanas de Cocle, Estudio de Estructuras Agrarias y Analisis de la Reforma Agraria*. Panama: Direccion General de Planificacion y Administracion de la Presidencia, 1970.

________. *El Hombre y la Tierra en Nata de 1700 a 1850*. Panama: Editorial Universitaria, 1971.

________. "Desarraigo y Migracion de Polbaciones en Panama. 1950-1960." *Anales de Ciencias Humanas* 1 (December 1971).

________. Presencias Imperialistas y Dependencia Istmica en al Segunda Mitad del Siglo XIX. Panama: Universidad de Panama, May 1973.

________. "La Formacion de Estructuras Economicas y Sociales en el Istmo de Panama: El Siglo VIII Colonial (1740-1850)." Tareas, no. 39 (July-September 1977), pp. 61-74.

________. "Negros y Esclavos en la Epoca Colonial en Panama--El Problema de la Apreciacion de la Presencia Cultural Africana en el Istmo." Unpublished manuscript, 1980.

________, and Pitti, Ana. "La Propiedad de la Tierra en Panama." Dialogo Social, no. 21 (October 1970).

Jaffe, A. J. "Economic Development and the Growth of the Male Working Force of Panama 1950-1960." American Journal of Economics and Sociology 25 (July 1966):297-306.

Jaguaribe, Helio, et al. La Dependencia Politica-Economica de America Latina. Mexico: Siglo XXI, 1970.

Jalee, Pierre. The Pillage of the Third World. New York: Monthly Review Press, 1968.

________. El Imperialismo en 1970. Mexico: Siglo XXI, 1971.

Jimenez Camacho, Francisco. El Impuesto Sobre la Renta en la Republica de Panama 1967. Mexico: Secretaria de Hacienda y Credito Publico, Administracion General de Impuestos al Ingreso, 1967.

Johnson, John. The Military and Society in Latin America. Stanford: Stanford University Press, 1964.

Jovane, Juan. "El Centro Financiero Internacional de Panama." Tareas, no. 36 (August-October 1976), pp. 47-58.

________, et al. Inflacion, Recesion, Perspectivas y Soluciones; Analisis de la Coyuntura Economica. Panama: Instituto Panameno de Estudios Laborales, 1974.

Juntas Comunales y el Proceso Revolucionario. Select newspaper clippings (1972-74) found in National Library in Panama.

Kahl, Joseph A. Modernization, Exploitation and Dependency in Latin America: Germani, Gonzalez, Casanova and Cardoso. New Brunswick: New Jersey Transaction Books, 1967.

"Kidnapping of Priest in Panama Is Called Threat to Canal Talks." New York Times, September 27, 1971.

King, Thelma. El Problema de la Soberania en las Relaciones entre Panama y los Estados Unidos. Panama, n.d.

LaFeber, Walter. The Panama Canal: The Crisis in Historical Perspective. New York: Oxford University Press, 1978.

Lagos, Medoro, and Miranda, Otilio. El General Volvio: 15 de Diciembre de 1969. Panama, 1969.

Latin American Report and Weekly Report. Latin American newsletters published in London.

Legarra, Mons. Martin, Bishop of Santiago de Veraguas. "Palabras Pronunciadas Sobre el Caso de Hector Gallegos por Television el Jeuves." Panama, June 17, 1971.

________. Letter to Lic. Juan Materno Vasquez, minister of government and justice, Panama, July 27, 1971.

Lehman, David, and Zemelman, Hugo. El Campesinado: Clase y Conciencia de Clase. Buenos Aires: Ediciones Nueva Vision, 1972.

Leis, Raul Alberto. Cooperativismo: Que Le Paso? Panama: Centro de Estudios Latino Americanos "Justo Arosemena," 1979.

Letter sent on January 8, 1969, by all the appointed civilian ministers offering resignation to Col. Jose M. Pinilla Fabreta, president of the Provisional Junta and to Col. Bolivar Urrutia Parrilla, member of the Provisional Junta.

Lieuwen, Edwin. Arms and Politics in Latin America. New York: Praeger, 1960.

Liss, Sheldon. The Canal: Aspects of the United States-Panamanian Relations. Notre Dame: University of Notre Dame Press, 1968.

Long, Norman. "Structural Dependency, Modes of Production and Economic Brokerage in Rural Peru." In Beyond the Sociology of Development: Economy and Society in Latin America and Africa, edited by Ivar Oxaal, et al. London: Routledge & Kegan Paul, 1975, pp. 253-82.

Looney, Robert E. The Economic Development of Panama. New York: Praeger, 1976.

Lopez Guevara, Carlos Alfredo. "Un Canal Sin Zona del Canal." Paper presented at the Municipal Palace in Colon, July 31, 1974.

MacEoin, Gary. "Church-State Rift Grows in Panama." National Catholic Reporter, January 7, 1972.

Mack, Gerstle. The Land Divided (A History of the Panama Canal and Other Isthmian Canal Projects). New York: Alfred Knopf, 1944.

Magdoff, Harry. Age of Imperialism: The Economics of U.S. Foreign Policy. New York: Monthly Review Press, 1969.

Mahon, Leon T. "Preguntas y Respuestas sobre los Nucleos Familiares". San Miguelito, August 15, 1971.

Manduley, Julio. Panama: Acerca de la Estructura, la Coyuntura y las Perspectivas. Panama: Centro de Estudios Latinoamericanos "Justo Arosemena," 1978.

Marchosky, Euseblo. "Asamblea Representativa?" Dialogo Social, no. 54 (March 1974).

Matutino. Newspaper.

Mauro Marini, Ruy. Dialectica de la Dependencia. Mexico: Serie Popular, Era 22, 1973.

McCain, William D. The United States and the Republic of Panama. New York: Russell and Russell, 1965.

McGrath, Mons. Marcos G. "Nota Prensa Distribuida en al Conferencia de Prensa Celebrada en la Ciudad de Bogota, en la Sede del Consejo Episcopal Latinamericano." Press release distributed to a press conference held in Bogota at the Latin

American Episcopal Council, August 4, 1971, 12:30 p.m.

Medrano de Gonzales, Eneida. "La Inversion Directa Extranjera en Panama." _Anales de Ciencias Humanas_ 1 (December 1971).

Mejia Robledo, Alfonso. _Quien es Quien en Panama: Diccionario Biografico y Bibliografico de Personalidades Actuales_. Medellin: Editorial Bedout, 1949.

Mellander, Gustavo. _United States in Panamanian Politics_. Danville, Ill.: Interstate Printers and Publishers, 1971.

Mendez Vega. _Demostenes, El Panamenismo y Su Doctrina_. Panama, 1963.

Menjivar, Rafael, ed. _La Inversion Extranjera en Centroamerica_. Costa Rica: Editorial Universitaria Centroamericana, 1974.

Merril, William C., et al. _Panama's Economic Development: The Role of Agriculture_. Iowa State University Press, 1975.

Miami Herald.

Miliband, Ralph. _El Estado en la Sociedad Capitalista_. Mexico: Ediciones Siglo XXI, 1976.

Miner, Dwight Carroll. _The Fight for the Panama Route (The Story of the Spooner Act and the Hay Herran Treaty)_. New York: Columbia University, 1940.

Montalvan, Jorge. "Democracia, Representantes de Corregimientos y Liberacion Nacional." _Revista Nacional de Cultura_, no. 4 (July-September 1976), pp. 77-89.

Movimiento de Unificacion Nacional, Desarrollo y Orientacion. "Hacia una Reestructuracion del Pais: Comunicado de la Cuarta Linea." October 1968.

________. "Proposal for Proportional Representation by Amending the Electoral Code." November 1968.

________. "Exposicion de Principios y Objetivos, Centro de Produccion (CENTROCOOP) de Nuevo Veranillo." n.d.

Munoz Pinzon, Armando. _La Huelga Inquilinaria de 1932_. Panama: Editorial Universitaria, 1974.

Navas, Luis. El Movimiento Obrero en Panama (1880-1914). Panama: Editorial Universitaria, 1974.

Nearing, Scott, and Freeman, Joseph. Dollar Diplomacy: The Classic Study of American Imperialism. New York: Modern Reader, 1969.

Nichols, Howard Harry. Military Government in the Panama Canal Zone. Norman: University of Oklahoma Press, 1931.

Nun, Jose. "A Latin American Phenomenon--The Middle Class Military Coup." In Latin America: Reform or Revolution, edited by James Petras and Maurice Zeitlin. New York: Fawcett World Library, 1968, pp. 145-85.

Nunez, Carlos. "Panama: El Reformismo de los Militares." Pensamiento Critico, no. 41 (June 1970), pp. 208-19.

________. "Exportacion de Capital en la Fase Premonopolista el Contrato del Ferrocarril de Panama de 1850." Tareas, no. 27 (December 1973-May 1974), pp. 71-82.

Nunez Soto, Orlando, and Guevara, Carmen. "Desarrollo y Contradicciones en el Proceso Panameno." Tareas, no. 41 (January-March 1978), pp. 25-64.

O'Donnell, Guillermo. "Apuntes Para una Teoria del Estado." Estudios Sociales Centroamericanos 7 (May-August 1978):177-219.

Organization of American States. Inter-American Economic and Social Council. Inter-American Committee on the Alliance for Progress. "Domestic Efforts and the Needs for External Financing for the Development of Panama." July-August 1973.

________. Inter-American Economic and Social Council, Inter-American Committee on the Alliance for Progress, CIAP Subcommittee on Panama. "Domestic Efforts and the Needs for External Financing for the Development of Panama." Washington, D.C., August 13-17, 1973.

________. Instituto de Ciencias Agricolas. IV Reunion Interamericana de Ejecutivos de Reforma Agraria. Panama, May 14-20, 1972.

________. Union Panamerica. La Viviendaen Panama. Washington, D.C., 1968.

Oxaal, Ivar; Barnet, Tony; and Booth, David. Beyond the Sociology of Development: Economy and Society in Latin America and Africa. London: Routledge & Kegan Paul, 1975.

Padelford, Norman J. The Panama Canal in Peace and War. New York, 1942.

Padilla, Solomon, and Vargas, Hugo. El Financiamiento Publico Externo en Panama y Sus Implicaciones Economicas. Panama: Centro de Estudios Latinoamericano "Justo Arosemena," 1978.

Palmer, D. S. "Revolution from Above: Military Government and Popular Participation in Peru 1968-1973." Ann Arbor, Michigan: University Microfilms, 1973.

"Panama." NACLA Latin America & Empire Report, vol. 8, no. 7 (September 1974).

Panama Canal. Personnel Regulation, governing conditions of employment of Panama Canal and Railroad Employees on the Gold Roll on the Isthmus, 1928.

Panama Election Factbook. Washington Institute for the Comparative Study of Political Systems, 1968.

PanCanal West Indian Employees Association. Annual Reports, 1927-1928 and 1942. Ancon Library, Canal Zone.

Partido del Pueblo. Hacia la Derrota de la Oligarchia y Imperialismo, Documento de la Conferencia Nacional sobre la Linea Electoral. Panama, March 11, 1978.

Pereira Burgos, Cesar. "Experiencias y Significacion del Movimiento de Trabajadores Bananeros de Bocas del Toro." Tareas, no. 4 (1961), pp. 26-44.

Pereira, Renato. Fuerzas Armadas y Politica. Panama: Ediciones Nueva Universidad, 1979.

Perez, Victor Manuel, and DeLeon Lerma, Rodrigo Oscar. El Movimiento de Accion Comunal en Panama. Panama: El Arte Tipografico, S.A., n.d.

Petras, James, and Zeitlin, Maurice. Latin America: Reform or Revolution? Greenwich, Conn.: Fawcett Premier Books, 1968.

Petras, James, et al. Cultivating Revolution: The United States and Agrarian Reform in Latin America. New York: Vintage Books, 1973.

Pippin, Larry. The Remon Era. Stanford: Institute of Hispanic American and Luso-Brazilian Studies, 1964.

Pitti, Dario Gonzales. Cuatro Discursos. Panama: Editoriales de la Voz del Poder Popular, 1976.

Porras, Demetrio. Veinte Anos de Luchas y Experiencias. Buenos Aires: Editorial Americalee, 1947.

Poulantzas, Nicos. Classes in Contemporary Capitalism. London: NLB, 1975.

Powell, John Duncan. Political Mobilization of the Venezuelan Peasant. Cambridge: Harvard University Press, 1971.

Priestley, George. "Encuesta Sobre la Organization y Participacion dentro de los Asentamientos." (This was a socioeconomic and political survey designed to be administered to nineteen asentamientos in five provinces. However, it was administered only to three asentamientos in the Baru district of Chiriqui.)

________. "A Decade of Panamanian Politics 1950-1960: A Study of Political Development." Unpublished, 1967.

________. "Security Council in Panama." Bayano 1 (March 1973):1.

________. "Labor Movements on the Panama Canal Zone: History, Structure and Goals." Paper presented informally to CUNY for funding, 1976.

________. "Race, Class and the Formation of the Panamanian Nation-State." Paper presented at the Second Conference on Black Cultural Identity in the Americas, Panama, March 1980.

________, and Maloney, Gerardo. "El Grupo Antillano en el Proceso Politico Panameno." Tareas, no. 33 (September-November 1975), pp. 11-27.

Proyecto Panama 71/521 (PAN-21). "Desarrollo y Planificacion; Capacitacion sobre Fases y Etapas de Formulacion de Proyectos Locales." Panama, December 1972.

Quijano, Anibal. Nationalism and Capitalism in Peru. New York: Monthly Review Press, 1971.

________, and Weffort, Francisco C. Marginalizacion y Dependencia. Costa Rica: Editorial Universitaria Centroamericana, 1973.

Quiros Guardia, Alberto. "La Lucha por la Soberania." Unpublished paper.

Real, Blay, and Lungo, Mario. "La Problematica Regional en Centroamerica." Estudios Sociales Centroamericanos, no. 23 (May-August 1979).

La Republica. Newspaper.

Ricord, Humberto. "El Tratado Remon-Eisenhower." Relaciones entre Panama y los Estados Unidos. Panama: Biblioteca Nuevo Panama, 1974, pp. 252-64.

________. "Jurisdiccion Laboral Panamena." Dialogo Social, no. 54 (March 1974).

________, et al. Panama y la Frutera: Una Batalla contra el Colonialismo. Panama: Editorial Universitaria de Panama, 1974.

Rijfkogel, Maria. "Sobre el Articulo XXXV del Tratado Mallarino-Bidlack." Relaciones entre Panama y los Estados Unidos. Panama: Biblioteca Neuvo Panama, 1974, pp. 105-14.

Robles, Winston. "El Hombre Frente al Poder." Dialogo Social, no. 54 (March 9, 1974).

Rodney, Walter. How Europe Underdeveloped Africa. London: Bogle-L'Ouverture and Tanzana Publishing House, 1972.

Rodriguez, Cesar A. Analisis Conceptual del Desarrollo de la Comunidad. Buenos Aires: Editorial ECRO, 1970.

Royo, Aristides. "Nueva Estructuras de Participacion." Paper delivered at the School of Dentistry of the University of Panama, March 25, 1974.

Russo Berguido, Alessandro. Horario de una Traicion. Panama, 1951.

Salamin, Marcel, and Salamin, Judith. Concepcion Oligarica de las Negociaciones entre Panama y los Estados Unidos. Panama, 1976.

"The San Miguelito Paper." Prepared by the priests of San Miguelito, January 20, 1964.

Schmitter, Philippe C., ed. Military Rule in Latin America, Function, Consequences and Perspectives. Vol. 3. Sage Research Progress Series on War, Revolution and Peacekeeping. New York, 1973.

Scott, Juan Felipe. Analisis de la Reforma Agraria Panamena, 1962-1968. Panama: Direccion General de Planificacion y Administracion de la Presidencia, 1970.

"Si Desaparezco No Me Busquen, Sigan el Trabajo." Dialogo Social (special edition), nos. 34-35 (May-June 1972).

Sintesis. Magazine.

Sisnett, Manuel Octavio. Belisario Porras o la Vocacion de la Nacionalidad. Panama, n.d.

"Sobre la Situacion Panamena." Sintesis, no. 1 (December 1977).

"La Sociologia en las Ciencias Sociales Panamenas." Paper presented by a group of Panamanian social scientists at I Congreso Centroamericano de Sociologia in Heredia, Costa Rico, April 22-27, 1974.

Soler, Ricaurte. Panama en el Mundo Americano, Programa Analitico-Alegato. Panama: Ediciones de la Libreria Cultural, 1971.

________. Clase y Nacion en Hispanoamerica. Panama: Siglo XIX, Ediciones de la Revista Tareas, 1975.

Sosa, Juan B., and Arce, Enrique J. Compendio de Historia de Panama. Panama, 1911.

Souza, Ruben Dario, et al. Panama 1903-1970: Nacion, Imperialismo, Fuerzas Populares y Oligarquia, Crisis y Camino Revolucionario. Santiago, 1970.

Stallings, Barbara. "Privatization and the Public Debt: U.S. Banks in Peru." NACLA Report on the Americas, 12 (July-August 1978):2-19.

Stavenhagen, Rodolfo. "Aspectos Sociales de la Estructura Agraria en Mexico." Revista de America Latina, January-March 1966.

________. Social Classes in Agrarian Societies. Garden City, N.J.: Doubleday, Anchor, 1975.

________, ed. Agrarian Problems and Peasant Movements in Latin America. Garden City, N.J.: Doubleday, Anchor, 1970.

Stein, Stanley, and Stein, Barbara. The Colonial Heritage of Latin America. New York: Oxford University Press, 1970.

Stepan, Alfred. The Military in Politics: Changing Patterns in Brazil. Princeton, N.J.: Princeton University Press, 1971.

Suarez Melo, Mario. Las Empresas Comunitarias Campesinas en Panama. Bogota: Instituto Interamericano de Ciencias Agricolas de la OEA, April 1972.

Tareas. Newspaper.

Taylor, Paul. Evaluacion del Programa de Desarrollo Comunal Urbano de Panama. Panama: Ministerio de Trabajo y Bienestar Social, September 1968.

Tomes, R. Panama 1855: An Account of the Panama Railrod of the Cities of Panama and Aspinwall, with Sketches of Life on the Isthmus. n.d.

Torres-Rivas, Edelberto. Interpretacion del Desarrollo Social Centroamericano. Costa Rica: Editorial Universitaria Centroamericana, 1973.

________. "Problemas del Desarrollo y la Dependencia Centroamericana." Revista Mexicana de Sociologia 13 (April-June):223-45.

Torrijos, Omar. La Batalla de Panama. Buenos Aires: Editorial Universitaria de Buenos Aires, 1973.

________. Mi Pueblo. Argentina: Cuadernos de la Linea, 1974.

________. Nuestra Revolucion: Discursos Fundamentales del General Omar Torrijos Herrera, Jefe de

Gobierno de la Republica de Panama. Panama: Departamento de Informacion, Ministerio de Relaciones Exteriores, 1974.

Turner, Domingo H. "Apunte Sociologico de la Politica Panamena." *Loteria*, no. 56 (1960).

United Nations. *United Nations Statistical Abstract*. 1969, 1970, 1971, 1972.

University of Panama. Administrative Board. "Manifesto a la Nacion." October 14, 1968.

University of Tennessee. "The University and Foreign Aid: Republic of Panama." Report to AID covering contract operations in Panama, 1950-1964.

Urriola, Oronel M. *Dialectica de la Nacion Panamena: Periodo Republicano*. Bogota: Editorial Colombia Nueva, 1972.

Valdes, Manuel M. *Las Intervenciones Electorales en Panama*. Panama, 1932.

Vasconi, Tomas Amadeo. *Gran Capital y Militarizacion en America Latina*. Mexico: Ediciones Era, Serie Popular, 1978.

Vasquez, Juan Materno. *El Pais por Conquistar: La Tesis del Pais Integral*. Bogota: Internacional de Publicaciones, 1974.

Velasquez, Jorge T. *Banco y Desarrollo Economico en Panama*. Mexico, 1970.

La Verdad Socialista.

Villarreal, Armando. *Situacion y Tendencias del Analfabetismo en Panama*. Panama, 1974.

Voguel, Leon. The Gallegos Case in Panama: Why His Abuction is Really No Mystery." Unpublished.

Wall Street Journal.

Wallace, John F. "Our Colonial Empire: The Republic of Panama and Canal Zone." *World Today* 14 (1908):359-67.

Westerman, George W. *The Problem of West Indian Offspring in Panama: A Study of Relationship of Ethnic and Cultural Groups in a Cosmopolitan Setting*. Panama, 1944.

________. "Gold Men and Silver Men." The Crisis, December 1947.

________. The West Indian Worker in the Canal Zone. Panama: National Civic League, 1951.

Wolf, Eric. Peasant Wars of the Twentieth Century. New York: Harper & Row, 1969.

Wood, Bryce. Urban Housing in Panama. Panama: The Institute for Economic Development, May 1955.

________. The Making of the Good Neighbor Policy. New York: W.W. Norton, 1961.

Yau, Julio. El Canal de Panama: Calvario de un Pueblo. Madrid, 1972.

Zapelock, William. "El Caso del Padre Hector Gallegos en Panama." Bogota, June 23, 1971.

Zentena, Raul Benitez. Clases Sociales y Crisis Politica en America Latina. Mexico: Siglo XXI, 1977.

Documents, Decrees, and Laws of the Republic of Panama

Asamblea Nacional Constituyente de Representantes. Memoria. September 11-October 11, 1972.

Asamblea Nacional de Representantes de Corregimientos. Diario de los Debates. 1972, 1973, 1974.

Codigo de Trabajo de 1972.

Comision de Legislacion. La Nueva Constitucion Politica de 1972, no. 3.

________. Experiencia Panamena, Las Juntas Comunales: Filosofia, Estructura y Concrecion Politica como Agente de Cambio, no. 5 (1977).

Comision Nacional de Energia Electrica, Gas y Telefonos. Memoria. 1973-1974.

Comision de Reforma Agraria. "Plan de Accion en la Provincia de Veraguas." 1970. Mimeographed.

________. Direccion de Desarrollo Campesino. Informe de Actividades (Primer Semestre 1972).

________. Direccion de Planeamiento y Programacion. Program de Trabajo, Ano 1971.

Decreto de Gabinete No. 147. June 3, 1969. (Creates National Directorate for Community Development)

Decreto de Gabinete No. 222. July 16, 1969. (Outlines functions of National Directorate for Community Development)

Decreto de Gabinete No. 258. July 30, 1970. (Creates the Experimental District of San Miguelito)

Decreto de Gabinete No. 401. December 29, 1970. Salud Igual para Todos.

Direccion de Estadistica y Censo. Censos Nacionales de 1970. Septimo Censo de Poblacion-Tercer Censo de Vivienda, May 10, 1970. Compendio General de Poblacion, vol. 3.

________. Censos Nacionales de 1970, Resultados Generales Crecimiento de la Poblacion de la Republica: Censo 1911-1970. Septimo Censo de Poblacion y Tercer Censo de Vivienda.

________. Compendio Estadistico: Provincia(s) de Panama, Colon, Cocle, Herrera, Los Santos, Veraguas, Bocas del Toro, Chiriqui y Darien. Individual volumes per province.

________. Estadisticas Vitales. Panama, 1974.

________. Panama en Cifras. 1968-1978.

Direccion General de Desarrollo de la Comunidad. Memoria. 1970.

________. Primer Encuentro de Dirigentes Indigenas. 1971.

________. Memoria. 1971-1972.

________. Memoria. 1973.

________. Memoria. 1974.

Direccion General de Planificacion y Administracion. Informe Economico 1970.

________. Departamento de Personal. Estructura de Salarios en Panama. 1969.

________. Departamento de Planificacion. Estudios Sectoriales: Diagnostico Sector Industrial. November 1971.

________. Departamento de Planificacion. Anexo: Presupuesto de Inversiones Publicas. 1971.

Direccion de Information y Relaciones Publicas. Directorio Estatal. 1973.

Gobierno Nacional. Plan Operativo del Gobierno Nacional para 1974 Panama. Panama: Impresora Nacional, 1974.

Ley No. 413. 1970. (Regulates and promotes export industry)

Ley No. 172. 1971. (Regulates and promotes export industry)

Ley No. 12. January 25, 1973. (Creates Ministry of Agricultural Development)

Ley No. 1. October 19, 1973. (Reglamento Interno de la Asamblea Nacional de Representantes de Corregimientos)

Ministerio de Desarrollo Agropecuario. Plan Sectorial de Produccion Ano 1974-75.

________. "Empresas Multiples Agrarias." 1974. Unpublished.

________. Direccion de Reforma Agraria. Informe de Actividades de 1973.

Ministerio de Educacion. Relaciones Entre Panama y los Estados Unidos, Papers of Primer Seminario Nacional de Historia de las Relaciones entre Panama y los Estados Unidos. Panama: Biblioteca Nuevo Panama, 1974.

________. Direccion Nacional de Planeamiento y Reforma Educativa. Los Corregimientos en el Desarrollo Socio-Economico de Panama. 1974.

Ministerio de Obras Publicas. Memoria. 1973-1974.

Ministerio de Planificacion y Politica Economica. Informe Economico 1974. Panama: Litho Impresora S.A., 1974.

________. Memoria. 1974.

________. *El Tecniquito, Boletin Informativo*, vol. 2, no. 19 (May 1974).

________. *Plan Nacional de Desarrollo (1976-1980)*, vol. 1 (1976).

________. *Informe Economico 1977*. October 1977.

Oficina de Regulacion de Precios. *Informe Anual*. 1974.

Panama en Cifras. November 1974.

Tribunal Electoral. *Elecciones Populares para Escoger Representantes de Corregimientos 6 de Agosto de 1972*. Organizacion Electoral, Manual de Procedimientos.

________. *Legislacion Electoral (Elecciones Populares para Escoger Representantes de Corregimientos), 6 Agosto, 1972*.

Zona Libre de Colon. *Memoria*. 1973-1974.

Index